Thanks
support!
[signature] Philp 3:8-1

From Cult to Christ

———+———

A Guide to Warning and Truth

By Craig Kuhn

PRESS

Table of Contents

———+———

v

—†—

*T*his work is dedicated to Jesus Christ for dying on the Cross for me and to my dear family who have never stopped believing in me: my dear bride, Janey, and my two boys Benjamin and Caleb. It is also dedicated to my mother and sister who have supported my dreams and me over the years, even though I've caused each to shed a tear or two.

My basic premise with this book is to educate and warn. It is also meant to be a helpful guide for well-meaning Christians—whether they are parents, church elders, pastors, teachers, believers of any kind—in making sure they cast God, and His Son, our Savior and Lord, Jesus Christ, in the light of truth and love rather than the light of vengeance and pain. And to remind us that we're saved by grace, not by our works.

I will do my best in this work in not mentioning specific organizations that are, frankly put, cults. I will instead convey my experience of over 16 years. I will elaborate on their fabrications, deceit, and the ruin they have caused in many lives, mine included. At this writing I am very grateful for my Lord and my God. I fell on my knees at the foot of His cross on the floor of my shag-carpeted family room, all alone and sobbing. There, I faced my situation with truth and honesty, and begged Him to show me how to get out.

What you are about to read is more of a journey than an account, it is a story rather than a biography. It's about how I first understood there is a God, how I got disillusioned at a very young age by well-meaning Christians, how I knew God, Jesus Christ and the Bible were all related, how I searched every where but the church (since I had rejected it) and how I fell prey to the promises, empty as they were, of an organization in which I spent many years and one divorce. Not to mention a significant amount of money.

Then it turns to escape, how I got out, and how God was intimately involved through my whole life but especially at a very great crossroads of life, especially the crossroad on the shag carpet.

May this book bless and educate you, but mostly, may it bring glory to our God and Savior.

At no point is this meant to be a "kiss and tell" kind of book, but there are real life stories that need to be conveyed to express both the thought processes of the victim and the tactics employed by the cult. Only with permission have I used real names, otherwise, all names are fictitious even though the situations portrayed are real.

And finally, I want to thank my many friends who helped with this work, especially Rod and Beth, for your tireless editing; Randy, for editing and inspiration; Barry, for being my Pastor; Clark, for your advice; Lynda, for your well-stated comments; and of course, Janey, who never stopped believing in me, edited every word several times, and was and is my number one cheerleader —I love you!

CHAPTER ONE

How and Where it All Began

—+—

"You made us for yourself, and our hearts find no peace until they rest in you."
—*St. Augustine, Confessions*

I remember it with shocking clarity. There I was, in the back seat of my Dad and Mom's blue Chevy Bellaire. Dad was driving, Mom in the passenger seat, my sister in the back seat behind Mom, and I was behind Dad. It was the first weekend after my fifth birthday, and we all piled into the car and drove from Salem to Portland to be with my Mom's parents, Bonca and Grammy, and to open presents in celebration of my birthday.

We gathered in their roomy day-light basement with the charcoal illustrations on the wall, drawn up there by my Grandpa, as he was always illustrating something back in those days before his hands became shaky. I don't remember all the presents I received but I do remember getting a mustard-yellow Hot Wheels track, a bunch of new little Hot Wheels cars, and a car carrier that looked like a mag wheel with a white-lettered tire. We ate cake, sang the "Birthday Song", played and talked. Somehow, as the shadows grew longer and night descended, we loaded back up in the Bellaire and headed south on Interstate 5 toward home. At that time the speed limit was 70 miles per hour, which meant Dad was probably doing about 75. A little more than halfway home I was gazing out my side window at the full moon.

That's when it happened. That's when God introduced Himself to me.

Looking at the moon, dreamily wishing I was an astronaut on an Apollo mission, a thought popped into my head like no other thought that had ever popped into my head before. The thought was; put your seat belt on. In fact, it repeated itself and was sort of like a small voice inside my head saying, "Put your seat belt on." I was much too young to find that creepy, and besides, with the voice came a warmth that said I was safe. So, instead, I found it strangely comforting even though no one in my family actually said anything out loud.

Now, keep in mind, this was in 1967 when virtually no one wore seat belts. For some reason, people hadn't put together that wearing seat belts would save more lives. We were still thinking back then that they were nothing more than a nuisance wrinkling our clothes and cutting into our hipbones. Plus, we may be trapped in the car if we crashed into a lake (even though there were no lakes anywhere near our travels) or if the car suddenly burst into flames, which, of course, only happened in the movies.

But I put them on anyway, primarily because I felt a warmth and a concern from the voice that made the urgency of obedience unquestionable.

That's when the second major thing happened.

At 75 miles an hour, the rear tire on my side of the car blew out. At that speed, our car spun out of control; how odd that on an otherwise crowded two-lane freeway, no cars were near us. Well, as the car was spinning with Dad fighting gallantly to regain control, all my family members bounced around the car —banging into the sides of the car, bumping their heads against the windows, grabbing stiff-armed onto whatever was in front of them —while I sat relatively still watching the moon and stars spin away to be followed by swirling chalky dust...then stillness. All was quiet for a moment, the lights on the dashboard were fading but the headlights were shining stiff shafts through the chalky dust now beginning to settle in on and around the car. Mom frantically began checking on my sister and me while Dad struggled to start the engine that was stubbornly groaning but not turning over. Suddenly, it dawned on both my Mom and me that had I not been belted, I probably would have catapulted through the windshield to my instant and very messy death. At the very least, since I was a very small five-year-old, I would have bounced all over the car, being very badly beaten and hurt if not killed.

So it is true...seat belts save lives.

So does God, but that hadn't dawned on me quite yet.

Well, I'm not sure exactly what Dad did (I'm not sure he was either), but the car landed safely in the shoulder, perpendicular to the freeway and on the opposite side from where we started to spin. The front of the car was pointing toward the road, and the rear settled into a ditch running the length of the shoulder. The car was in eerie stillness, all the lights were still on as our headlights were shooting across the two-lane freeway, but the engine was dead and no one said a word while pale dust swirled around us, still aglow from the dimming headlights. Then, like a dark cloud ready to drop its load, I burst into tears. The immensity of what had just happened, and how my life was just saved from death, started to fall upon my little brain like a cloudburst of rain in a dry Willamette Valley August.

As I sobbed in big, chest-heaving sobs, my sister placed her hands reassuringly on my shoulders, squeezing them now and then to remind me that our little family of four was still alive, and still together. As she squeezed my shoulders and cars whizzed by us, all kinds of thoughts swirled in my brain, but weren't quite gelling just yet. How is it no cars collided with ours as we spun around the two lanes? What kept our car from rolling over or shooting through the meridian into the on-coming traffic? How did it come to land so gently on the shoulder? And Who, or What, told me to put on my seat belts?

Little did I know, but my quest for God had just begun.

While I was still bawling and my sister was still comforting me, some people stopped to see if we needed help. Well, we couldn't drive the car without the spare tire and the rear of the car was so deep in the ditch, my Dad couldn't use his jack. So, in a word, we were stuck, and yes, we did need help (cell phones were still Star Trek gadgets). Before they stopped, though, I'm sure my Dad, as stoic as he was, must have been worrying himself sick on the inside about how he was going to get his family home late at night with a long way to go, hitchhiking wasn't exactly his specialty, especially with a 12 year old daughter and a five year old son. But, he didn't have too long to worry as a four door sedan pulled over in the shoulder just ahead of where we were all clustered in the dust at the side of the road.

I guess normally this wouldn't be such a big deal, some folks pulling over and doing a good Samaritan kind of deed. But in this case, of all the people who had passed us on the freeway, the couple that stopped were not only from Salem, but they actually lived in our neighborhood as well.

The guy said he would give us a lift but that he could also stop and call for a tow truck. He and Dad talked over their various options, finally deciding that the couple would take Mom, my sis and me home while also pulling into a truck stop to call for a tow truck, and Dad would wait on the side of the road with the car and all my presents.

It was weird leaving my Dad standing on the shoulder of the road, with the rest of us pulling away toward home with strangers in a strange car, but somehow we knew we were safe and that Dad would be fine, he'd just get home later than the rest of us, that's all. I remember waving good-bye to him as he waved back, the kind of wave that said "I love you" even though he rarely actually said the words, somehow, with my Dad, I just knew, we all just knew.

I don't remember much discussion on the ride home, just a continual re-counting of what happened and how "lucky" we were. I especially don't remember any talk about God, but for some reason, I didn't feel like we were lucky, I didn't know how to describe what I was feeling back then, but now I would describe it more as an elusive sense of destiny. The blow-out may have been an accident, but then, maybe not, but the fact that the blow-out resulted in no injuries and little property damage, spoke to me that more than just chance was involved.

I don't pretend to be a God expert, but I do know enough about God to understand that we really know very little about Him. So maybe the whole blowout experience was meant as a message to my family, or maybe just me, but whichever the case, it wasn't the first such message to ring through my family, but that's another story.

CHAPTER TWO

Black Dots and Flannel-Graphs from Hell

———+———

"Although I am an unworthy and condemned man, my God has given me in Christ all the riches of righteousness and salvation without any merit on my part."
—Martin Luther, *Treatise on Christian Liberty*

We were not a church-going family, especially since my Dad really had little respect for churches or church people, so the blowout experience just continued lingering on the fringes of my consciousness without much nurturing. But yet, it was never far off in my thinking either. Every so often I would recall the experience and ponder what that warmth was, who or what that voice was, and the same answer I came to again and again was it had to be God. I remember when I was young I also would stand outside at night, gazing up into a cloudless and moonless sky, marveling at the lighted expanse above me. I used to wonder many things about space and about the universe, but I always thought it had to have an intelligent design behind it and I never bought that it was nothing more than a cosmic accident. And if it was an accident, then who caused the accident to even occur? Who put the stuff causing the accident into each other's way? No one, not then and not now, can answer those questions scientifically. Therefore I surmised that all had to come from God, just as that inner warmth had.

So even without going to a church, I had an ebbing and flowing interest in Who and What God was all about. In fact, I would describe it more as a continual longing in the depths of my soul, a longing compelling me on a continuing quest for answers, a deep drive to fill that "God-shaped hole" in the bottom of my soul. A longing that kept telling me there was more to this life than just what I saw or felt; more to life than just eating, sleeping and going to school or work. Over the years, as this book will attest, I've placed much in that hole to fill it, only to have it leak out again and again, staining my very soul.

As I grew older and deeper into my most impressionable years, I quickly discovered, as so many of us do, many people's perspectives on God are not only skewed, they're wrong, bordering on evil. Not a good combination for an impressionistic pre-teen. And boy, are some of these perspectives damaging and hurtful.

Have you ever heard of God putting black dots on your soul? Well hang on, here's a doozy!

I remember one autumn morning, walking to school with a friend of mine; he was part of a big Christian denomination that I thought had an inside track on God. I was about twelve, and in the seventh grade and I was beginning to discover other things about life, things like heavy metal music, girls, and drugs. Anyway, my friend, Paul, was a known churchgoer so I naturally thought he knew a thing or two about God. I figured if one went to church every Sunday, they were most likely learning truths about God by reading their book, the

Bible. I later learned that many churches hardly even refer to the Bible; to them it's more of a decoration than life's manual for living. I further learned that these same churches had a strong propensity to teach that God was whatever you wanted Him to be, sort of a pre-packaged deity, placed on the shelf only to be brought down if you needed someone to blame or needed some sort of spiritual 9-1-1 call for help. He wasn't a constant companion or even a very present help in times of need, He was often the reason you had need because He was a God toying with people's lives, a God of vengeance, a God of wrath, and a God you wanted to cower from, not enter into relationship with Him.

I hadn't yet discovered all this at twelve, but I was beginning to. Thus, I was beginning to get my biggest disillusionment about God from the very people entrusted to carry His message of salvation and deliverance —Christians.

So I asked Paul about God.

"So what's God like," I asked innocently, expecting something about love and light. Instead, here's what I got:

"He's a vengeful God."

My mouth gaped open as I asked incredulously, "What do you mean 'vengeful'?"

"Well, you know, He punishes people when they do bad things."

"What sorts of bad things?"

"Let's see," said Paul, warming to my questions. After all, he was having a chance to witness for Christ, right? "Sins and stuff like that. Things like stealing or lying or killing people. Or cussing, my dad does that a lot!" And he smiled at me, but I didn't smile back.

"I haven't killed anybody, but that other stuff," I paused, looking down at the sidewalk, trying not to step on a crack, "I've done all those other things."

"Then you've sinned," said Paul simply.

That's that, I thought to myself, I've sinned. Now how do I go about fixing that? Was I doomed? Was God going to punish me? If so, how? I was really worried, for just that morning, unbeknownst to my parents, I had cussed a little bit for some silly reason I couldn't remember, but I could remember I had uttered a word, that if heard by my folks, would have gotten me grounded —for quite a while, too!

"How does God punish people?" I didn't want to ask, but I had to, I had to know what to expect from God.

"The way I understand it," responded Paul, "He places black dots on your soul up in heaven. When you get enough black dots, He kills you."

That rocked me to my core. The implications of this were staggering to me. How could that warm and kind voice telling me to put my seat belt on be the same source placing black dots on people's souls and then killing them for it? How could this God, whom I thought was supposed to be loving, be doing something like that? How could I worship a God I cowered from? How could I trust my heart to the very Being that was going to crush it?

Was this the God I was questing for, the god of black dots? What was Jesus Christ all about then? How did the Bible fit into all this?

I didn't say anything else for the rest of that walk. Arriving at school and pushing open the heavy chrome door, I remember thinking that I was beginning to fear the God I was searching for.

Paul and I remained friends until his family moved away. However, we never again talked about God. But there were certainly many others willing to take his place, with equally distorted views.

One summer, probably the one right after the black dot discovery, a friend of my mom's was putting on a summer Bible teaching thing in her family room. The teaching was being sponsored by her church, which was connected to another prominent denomination, and intended to be a Sunday school brought to the neighborhood during the week, sort of like a "Bible in the hood" kind of thing. I think it met weekly, but I only went once.

Evidently Sunday school teachers were really into teaching stories using large boards covered with green flannel. The flannel-covered boards would be placed on an easel and then flannel cutout characters were placed on the flannel surface as illustrations supporting the story being told. This technique was called a flannel-graph and my friend's mom used this technique.

So, on a sunny summer afternoon, even though I'd rather be outside playing, there I was, staring at a green piece of cloth waiting for some sort of motivational message (I had never seen a flannel-graph before so I was slightly intrigued). But when that session ended, I didn't remember the actual story, yet I did remember having the very daylights scared out of me.

She taught about sin and going to hell, and about eternal torment, and the devil. I don't remember anything about love or light, or even Christ. There was nothing about the sacrifice of Christ on the cross on my behalf or of the atoning of His spilled blood, or the significance of the resurrection. I don't remember any prayer and she didn't even use her Bible and I never heard a word about salvation — I was again confronted with being a sinner deserving punishment but given no way out it. She talked about Revelation and the wrath of God, like He was just some kind of really ticked off old man wanting to get even with the universe — but I didn't know why he wanted to get even. I didn't know how it was my fault, but somehow I was bad and apparently destined for hell. So rather than being filled with hope, I was filled with despair.

I left her house that day feeling like I should be scared of my own shadow, like if I stepped on it that would be one more item on my long list of sins, one more black dot closer to the baseball bat of death. I think she meant well and her technique seemed to be one of trying to literally scare the hell out of me. What she actually accomplished, however, was to cause me to fear God even more —and to hide from the "religious" people, because all they did was talk about fear and torment: Religion was beginning to symbolize death rather than life to the fullest as Jesus promised in John chapter 10. I started realizing that between the black dots and going to hell, I was scared to learn any more about God. I was happier as an ignorant sinner and I figured my life would be easier if I remained ignorant, that if I didn't know any better then I couldn't get hurt. Fat chance! I later learned that ignorance is definitely not bliss when talking about final eternal destinations!

I was a sensitive and worrisome child, so this kind of message consumed me with guilt, shame and great fear! I started fearing that since there seemed to be no way out of my sinful state, what would keep me from getting worse? What if I started to get real bad, you know a criminal kind of bad? What or who could help me? Or was I doomed to the fate of the black dot god of hell and torment?

Even though I was consumed with fear and not even able to sleep, I never told my parents about this. Now that I'm in my forties and my earthly father is gone, my mother is shocked when I tell her these stories. But would my parents have known what to do with my quest for God and how to cease my worries of all I had heard so far? I'll never know, of course, but I do regret not talking to them. So I guess I would encourage each reader of this personal journey to talk about these issues with your parents. Or, if you're an adult, don't take one person's word for it but compare what they say against what trusted authors, or trusted wiser friends say. Better yet, compare it to what the Bible says. The point, however, is just don't keep it in. Discuss what you're hearing and thinking with others.

And if you're a parent, most certainly keep your lines of communication open with your children —whether or not you are going to church. But of course if you're not, why? There are plenty of good churches out there, churches that don't make you feel even more ashamed or guilt-ridden, but instead teach the healing and the releasing of Jesus (Matthew 11:28-30).

Also remember that you can always pray for God's wisdom (James 1:5), but more about that later. And, perhaps most importantly, read the Bible yourself. It is God's Word to us about His heart of love and deliverance for us. Had I actually read some Bible when I was younger, I may not have been so bound in fear. If you're new to the Bible, Psalms and Proverbs are good places to start, so are Ephesians and the Gospel of John.

It took two weeks after that teaching before I could sleep soundly again, and years before I again openly resumed my quest for God. When I did resume my quest, I only ran into more dead-ends, but this time, the dead ends were in the churches themselves.

CHAPTER THREE

What Went Wrong in
the Local Church

———+———

*"...that he might perform all his actions for the love
of God."*
— Brother Lawrence, *The Practice of
the Presence of God*

"No man can tame the tongue."
— *James 3:8a*

I was not raised in what you'd call a Christian home. In
fact, if asked what our religion was, my Mom would
usually say Presbyterian, (even though we'd never been
in a Presbyterian church) and my Dad would say agnostic.
We never answered that we were Christian or that we even
acknowledged Jesus Christ. My family was not mean or
abusive, and we had no huge life-catastrophes many children face (including my own with a divorce), but we weren't
God-fearing in any way either. We were law-abiding,

strongly self-sufficient, and solidly middle class. Yet we never prayed, never opened a Bible, and my Dad was especially hostile toward churches and church people; "those darn religious people" he would say (only he would use a different 'd' word than 'darn'). "They're nothing but a bunch of hypocrites." Then he'd go on and complain about how they're always begging for money. "They don't care about God, they only want your money" was a common lament in our home. Dad would point at the TV and say, "look, they just beg for money, that's all they do."

Unfortunately, as I grew older, I found my Dad was more right than he was wrong, and not just being critical. Christian kids in my high school would call me "heathen" since I never went to church. They didn't reach out to me or offer me any sort of morsels of interest for Christ. They just called me "heathen" yet wanted to go to the same parties I went to. But with their words, I thought, "wow, if that's what Christ thinks of me, then I have no shot with Him anyway, so why bother!" As we all learn later in life, words do indeed hurt.

As a young child, I was sensitive and hugely susceptible to what people said and did to me. I was also small for my age, so I was made fun of a lot and picked on a lot. (Why is it groups of bullies pick one person to beat on, and that person is usually a runt and incapable of fighting back? Aren't those guys really just cowards and hugely insecure in themselves?) I don't really remember ever adopting a victim mentality or throwing huge poor-me-pity-parties, but I do remember wondering if there was some peace and acceptance somewhere in this harsh world.

I also worried a lot. I used to lie awake at night worrying about the most horrific types of things — things like me committing horrible crimes or horrible accidents happening to my family and me. And nothing stopped the worrying. So I used to fantasize about some miracle cure coming along to give me relief — a doctor, a pill, a shot, anything. But of course, nothing came. It just seemed I was hard-wired to worry, even about the most absurd things. And with the worry came the companion sicknesses that usually tear at your gut.

Since my experience with the blowout, I did still periodically wonder about God. Perhaps there was acceptance and relief there. Perhaps God's "bigness" wouldn't be harmful to my smallness. I remembered the strong sense of warmth and peace I had in that experience and, as stated earlier, I had unknowingly started a quest for God. Maybe God could give me peace. Maybe God would accept me for who I am.

But being so sensitive and susceptible made it a dangerous quest. With a kind word and polite gesture, I was duped.

My first exposure to churches was really with neighbors who were, as Dad labeled them, religious. When we moved to Salem, our neighbors were local churchgoers. They had three kids, two boys and one girl. I remember playing with the boy who was my age, and I remember the neighbors being nice, but I also remember them being awfully uptight and slightly paranoid. I remember that for them everything seemed to have some sense of evil about it and that they had weird ways of dealing with the world and its evil — they hid. They seemed to be avoiding the world more than participating in it. Their answer to life was to hide from it, not experience it. If they had enough big Bibles on the coffee table and enough crosses on the wall, they felt secure. But I never heard them ever utter anything about Jesus and His salvation and deliverance, I just heard smarmy religious phrases couched in a continual focus on how evil and dark the world was; in their world beauty seemed to only come in death because evil would be wiped out once we were all in heaven.

Now as I recall, when Jesus sent His disciples into the world, He never encouraged them to run away from it. In fact, the Great Commission in Matthew 28:18-20 is precisely about going into the world. How can the world ever learn about Jesus if those who know Him, hide from those who don't? And didn't Jesus Himself hang out with the Joe-Average dudes of His time? Check the Book out yourself. You will see there were prostitutes, tax collectors, soldiers, lepers, rulers, common folk, and even a thief. I'd say that's a pretty large representation of the world population, and Jesus went into that world —even when it cost Him His life. Even Romans 10:14-15 asks the rhetorical questions about how will people know or hear if no one opens their mouth to speak about the Good News of Jesus Christ.

When was the last time your life was truly at stake because you hung out with common folks? It's been a long time, I'm sure. In fact, it's probably been never, with the exception of a few missionaries in hostile territory, countries that horribly persecuted Christians, and some folks in real tough cities.

This principle is again reiterated in Acts 1:8 when Jesus tells His disciples they will be witnesses of Him "to the ends of the earth." I'm pretty sure the ends of the earth include suburban Salem. But still these neighbors hid from the world and sheltered their kids from cultural realities. Heck, my dad was a criminal defense attorney, so we saw more of the darker side of culture than we probably should have, while our neighbors cowered in fear of the slightest shadow on their door —no wonder we never had backyard barbecues together. A criminal defense attorney, whose clients included death row inmates, would definitely not mix well with a dad trying to shelter his family from the slightest hint of cultural reality!

So with all this clear instruction from Jesus Christ Himself, why did my religious neighbors cower in fear? Why did they hide from culture rather than truly try to impact it for Christ?

While I may never know the specifics for that family, I will say the general conclusion I was coming to regarding religious people and their churches was beginning to crystallize in one word: hypocrisy. What they really wanted was nothing more than a closed social circle of people who had a like religion and the same phobias and fears —it's like a weird group therapy thing that is totally enabling and with zero cure —we're in fear and that's okay —so let's not change let's keep our doors closed. Let's continue to hide behind the enclave of our four walls or our cloistered sanctuary and say our prayers while looking to heaven. They would act all "Christiany," but when it came to the real work of slogging through a muddy humanity, they'd bolt and run back to the enclave, boarding up the shutters of their souls and quenching the spirit in the process. (Ephesians 4:30 says we're not to quench the spirit, but instead give Him full access to our hearts and lives.)

I believe hypocrisy is the greatest evil in the Christian church today. I will continue to touch on this but will really explore it in more detail in a later chapter.

My next biggest example was with the "flannel graph" lady previously mentioned. Why do religious people think it's okay to scare the "hell" out of children? Do horror movies motivate people to fling open their doors and windows? Or do they instead motivate people to lock everything up real tight then go hide and shiver under the covers in a back room of the house? The answer is obvious. People get motivated to fear and to hide, so why is the logic of a "scary" flannel graph one that assumes after being scared by God that we'll then run to Him? Who would want to voluntarily run into the arms of a Hitler or Saddam Hussein? No one. Logic on its own clearly suggest we'd run the other way, and run fast, not looking back and certainly not returning to the scene.

How about another example? Stop and think for a moment about your most memorable dreams. Chances are they're nightmares. And what is the most memorable object of the nightmare? I doubt it's the clothes you were wearing. It's most likely the scary object itself. How does that apply here? Simple, scary stuff not only greatly impacts our memories, but also our thoughts about the subjects that scared us. This isn't rocket science, it's just psychology 101, better described as common sense. But for some reason common sense and religion don't co-exist.

Let's role-play for a minute. What do you think the following dialog will actually produce?

Church Lady: "All right kids, thanks for coming to today's Bible story. Now please sit down quietly criss-cross applesauce on the floor. Billy, stop pulling Maggie's cute little pony tails."

Billy: "Well, she started it!"

CL: "Fine. But I'll stop it. Okay. Who can tell me who this nice man is?" She places up on the green flannel graph a shepherd wearing a tunic and with long brunette hair, blue eyes and a smile.

Several children shout in semi-unison: "It's Jesus!!"

CL: "That's right, it's Jesus." (Usually pronounced JEEEzus.) "And if you don't believe in Him you're all gonna burn in hell! There'll be fire, and pain, and screams, forever; and you AND your families will all burn in hell if you don't accept Him right now! They'll be gnashing of teeth, black smoke, no way to breathe and your only way out is to accept Jesus." And as she's saying this she places on the flannel graph giant flames, black smoke, and pictures of people screaming. She finishes her presentation with a smile and waving her Bible around.

A loud ruckus is heard and all the kids run out of the house, screaming and crying.

Obviously this is very exaggerated, but I hope you get the point. Who are the children going to fear, the Church Lady or Jesus? Most likely both, but I bet they're more afraid of the one they think represents hell, and in this example it's Jesus. Imagine that, Jesus representing hell, but that's how I felt after these types of fire and brimstone sermons that were supposedly meant to entice me to accept Jesus. Why would I, or anyone else, accept the representative of hell?

Now how absurd is that? Jesus being connected to hell —who could think of such a thing. And yet, this approach is still being used this very day. Religious people are preaching in such a way that makes Jesus out to be a tyrant waiting to condemn people to hell. Such thinking would certainly drive people **away** from Jesus, not **to** Him.

Jesus Himself condemned this sort of thing. In fact, He even said it would be better for those turning people away from God to be cast in the sea than to lead a child astray (Matthew 18:5-6). And I think connecting Jesus to hell is certainly leading people astray. Further, Jesus encouraged children to come to Him and He welcomed them with love, not threats (Matthew 19:14-15). He is the invitation **out** of hell, not the doorway **to** it.

Next came experiences in actual churches. I want to be careful not to offend any denominations, but I do want to point out a few things about ritual and heart.

I remember going to this one church with a high school girlfriend. The church was a bigger one in town and part of a very prominent and rather ornate denomination. It was so ornate I called it pompous. But every Easter and Christmas Eve her family trotted off to church, I guess to make themselves feel better or something, because they too were not churchgoers. So to keep peace with my girlfriend and her family, I went with them to a midnight Christmas Eve thing. I think it was called Mass, but I didn't know what Mass meant other than just a mass of people crammed into a long, thin room with gold crosses at the front and hard, wooden benches for us to sit on.

The ceremony had a bunch of men in fancy silk robes and funny hats, carrying metal scepters, waving incense around or sprinkling water here and there. I heard no explanation why they wore such get-ups and I was later told that was just the way they did things. When I asked why, I was told not to question it, that's just the way it was. I thought to myself, "wow, I've really stumbled onto some secret society or something," or, more likely, they had no clue and were ashamed to admit it. As a side note, I strongly suggest you question anything you don't understand. If the answer doesn't come from the Bible Itself, you may want to be very cautious as to the motive behind the activity.

As the ritual progressed, they had Communion. There was no explanation as to what it was or why they were having it, but they did emphasize it was only for those who had been baptized. Well, I had never been baptized but I had accepted Christ, so I participated anyway. How would they know and what could they do about it anyway?

The "wine" was of course grape juice, but the bread was this funky white stuff like the bottom of a Styrofoam cup. I couldn't believe they were actually feeding me something that looked like carcinogen-carrying plastic! Well, I didn't want to offend them or embarrass myself, so, like everyone else, I stuck out my tongue so they could lay it on the tip. (That alone caused all kinds of hygiene questions to pop into my mind. Had they actually touched someone else's tongue? Ewww!). Then, as most people would do, I started to chew it — don't you usually chew bread, and wasn't this some sort of bread replacement? Well, evidently chewing was a taboo thing, for I received a very sharp elbow to my ribs and a "you're supposed to let it melt" sneer from my girlfriend. I thought that was funny. My Bible must have left out the part where Jesus said "take, let this melt on your tongue." Instead, my Bible has Him saying "take, eat." That usually requires chewing in my book.

Needless to say, my first Communion experience was way less than Jesus' broken body and shed blood. There was nothing about salvation, nothing about deliverance, and nothing about personal responsibility of being a Christ-follower. Instead, it was more of a shrouded ritual with lots of potential germ sharing and weird hocus-pocus. Simply put, there was no genuine heart of Christ, no warmth of love and compassion, no message of mercy for the sinner and no mention of eternal salvation. Rather, it was a cold, ritual-based, man-made mockery of the true essence of Jesus Christ.

I never went back to that church again. And that wasn't the last church I went to that felt more like a cold front than an oasis of God's warmth and love.

But let me give another example that just kind of freaked me out in general.

Even further back in my life, while I was in Junior High, I wanted to play church league basketball. That, of course, meant I had to go to a church. Being turned off about church by this time, I didn't really want to attend anywhere. I just wanted to play hoops. So I picked a large church in town that had been referred to me by a friend. I didn't want to go on Sunday —I figured that'd be too churchy —so I went to a Wednesday night service.

They played music (nothing like today's worship music) that had some beat to it. And at some point while everyone was standing and the music stopped, some guy just started blurting out what sounded like gibberish. Then someone else would yell out in English, then someone would go into another rendition of babbling gibberish. This went on for a few cycles and I thought these folks were freaks! There was no explanation of what was going on and why. It was just people freaking out like they were on drugs, or worse, possessed! And this was in a church!

That place was nuts in my mind, and guess what? I never went back there either. It was much later in life that I started learning about gifts of the Spirit and speaking in tongues and interpretation, but back then I had no clue about those things —it was just weirdo stuff to me. They apparently had no knowledge of doing things "in a fitting and orderly way" (I Corinthians 14:40).

Two last stories, but I think you get the point —there's a big difference between true heart and hypocrisy, genuine worship and putting on a show.

In high school I remember walking into this large gothic church. There were more men in robes (I couldn't tell if they were wearing slippers or not!), and a very suppressed, almost somber ambience. It felt more like a crypt or tomb, a place to go and die rather than to seek life. And Jesus came to give us life in abundance (John 10:10b). I don't remember the sermon but I do remember being cold and wanting to get the heck out of there and back into the fresh air and light.

In college I went to a Bible study. I thought maybe this'd be my answer. But as I got there, I was sorely disappointed. In preparation we were to read chapter three of Colossians. I thought it was a cool chapter, but I didn't really have much understanding of it, so I was looking forward to hearing more depth on it. Instead, the "leader" asked what each of us thought, so we all just sort of bumbled into some half-baked explanations. How'd he respond? "That all sounds good. Next week we'll..." That was it, nothing further, no learning, no teaching, not even any debate. I was hoping that he'd actually tell us the meaning of the chapter, explain to us the deeper truths of the chapter, in other words, I wanted some meat but came away with milk, or worse, pablum. We didn't even pray. I would have gotten as much if I just stayed home in the first place.

I'm sure he meant well. In fact, I'm sure all these folks meant well, but there's a big difference between meaning well and doing well. And I have even more examples: the priest and the Gospel of John; the corruptible religious girl; the uptight, judgmental puritan; and on and on.

The main point is what we do matters, but will it matter for or against God? That is the question I encourage people of any faith to ask themselves, especially if they're Christian leaders or teachers. We have no way of knowing how long or how deep our influence will reverberate, so it's important for our influence to reverberate and reflect Christ, the real Christ, not the manufactured one, not a man-made, watered down Jesus. Who knows if the seeds we sow into other people's lives will actually take root or not, but we need to make sure they're good seeds, seeds of love, deliverance and salvation, so that if they do take root, it will be the root of truth.

CHAPTER FOUR

What Went Right

———+———

"We have this hope as an anchor for the soul, firm and secure."

—Hebrews 6:19

Besides the blowout experience, something else went right in my life in my quest for God. And because of that my soul kept thirsting after that refreshing, even if it took decades. Thankfully, I finally got a taste of what my soul was so thirsting for.

It began with a trick and a lie to get me to take a youth group trip to Canada, but whether that was right or wrong, it was one of the most profound and lasting experiences of my entire life.

In Junior High, a boy named Steve who had been my best friend, moved up to Seattle. There he found Christ through a well-known organization that focuses on evangelizing and discipling youth.

I knew he had stumbled into this but I didn't spend much energy pursuing that with him since I had had my fill of black dots and flannel graphs —church people and church stuff was definitely not my bag.

Well, as time went on and summer rolled around, he invited me to go to "camp" with him for a week. I asked if this was a Christian camp and he said no, it wasn't. Good, I thought, I didn't want to spend a week of my summer with a bunch of Christians. Well, as it turned out, he lied, it was a Christian camp, with lots and lots of them to boot!

But, not knowing the truth, I went. As we boarded the ferry that would carry us across the Sound to a place called Malibu Island, I learned this was in fact a Christian camp. My first clue was there were a lot of people walking around carrying a Bible. My second clue was there were a lot of people standing in small groups, praying. I couldn't believe it, these kids were actually praying in public. Talk about uncool! Needless to say, I was ticked off— how could he have tricked me liked that? I thought he was a Christian? Did Jesus pull tricks on people?

I eventually got over it. In fact, I got over it before the ferry hit the island, which was about an eight-hour trip over all. But why did I get over it? Because the people were kind, they were genuine, they knew I wasn't a "believer" like them but they didn't condemn me for it. They welcomed unbe-lievers; they didn't try to scare or guilt me into believing. They just, if you can believe this, accepted me. I'll say it again in all caps this time —THEY ACCEPTED ME!!!! I didn't look up into conceited, self-righteous nostrils, I didn't hear anything about how to chew, or rather, suck Styrofoam or about being damned to hell or about black dots or flannel graphs, but I did hear about Jesus Christ. I heard about love, about mercy, about Him being an assistance, a very present help in times of need, and about salvation. I even heard about peace, peace of mind and peace of soul —two things I so longed for! That trip, whether my friend will have to answer for lying to me or not, is where I believe I first genuinely felt the Spirit move in my soul and where I eventually accepted Christ while walking through a lush Pacific Northwest forest. And there were no scary church ladies or men in funny hats and robes! Praise God!

I remember there was this large troubled kid, I think his name was Arne, but I'm not sure and I don't remember where he was from, but he was also accepted. That surprised me because he was one of those over-weight, very insecure bullies. He used his weight to push around the smaller and younger kids. But he was still loved and treated nicely and accepted. In fact, I got to the point to where I could accept him too, even though at the first of the week I thought he was a fat blow-hard, a big kid us little kids hated to be around because they always picked on us. I figured I'd either have to just completely avoid him or tattle on him so he'd leave me alone. But I knew I sure couldn't take him in a fight.

I later learned that he was in the midst of a shattered childhood and was only trying to protect his heart from more hurt. Bottom line, he was scared but was afraid to show it, so he acted tough and only beat on the kids he knew he could beat just like he was beaten. And early on I was one of his first targets. Have I already mentioned I was small for my age?

But we wound up becoming friends —and all I can say about that is it was a "God thing." Left to my own devices friendship would never have happened. I hated people who beat on us little guys.

This kid, though, was beat on in his own home!

Wow! And I thought my life was rough. I really wish I could remember his name, but through him I learned that sometimes-difficult people are difficult because they have been so badly treated, so badly hurt. They know no other life but the life of pain and are trying to hide or otherwise protect themselves from further pain and to hide from the shame that quickly followed in on pain's footsteps. They're also very vulnerable and fragile, sometimes easy prey for less than

Christ-like organizations (but more on that later). And here I am heaping upon that pain by ridiculing or avoiding him! Adding to his shame by not looking at him, talking to him or involving him.

Thank the Lord Almighty that His Spirit got a hold of me before I left that fir covered island, because I was able to let this kid know I considered him a friend who was helping me find Christ. In other words, he knew his life had significance, so much significance that he was helping a "desperate pilgrim" find the Lord he'd been seeking for so long. As we all know, significance is so important, and for the first time, this kid felt significant, not because of his fists, but because of his heart!

That's the Christ I was seeking, I didn't want the robe-covered, ritual laden, hypocritical religion. I wanted the real deal, I wanted Jesus Christ, and on that Island in the middle of Puget Sound, I found Him —or rather He found me.

And, yes, there was also a profound sense of peace and even joy welling up in my soul. Of course all of us Bible fans know these are two of the nine fruit produced by the Spirit (Galatians 5:22-23), but I hadn't become a Bible fan at that point in my life so I had no idea God actually promised peace or joy.

You see, as mentioned before, professional worriers raised me. So not only did I inherit their worry gene, I improved upon it. My improvement was so good that I worried about almost everything —my health, my school, my family. I worried I might become a criminal or a bum. I worried about all kinds of weird stuff— I even worried about my worrying. Simply put, I was a mess —and this was all before my mid-teens! I'm sure you understand why peace of mind was certainly one of the top items of relief on my quest for God. And Malibu Island was the first time I experienced mental peace for a sustained period. The problem was, when I came back home to Salem, I had no grounding in Christ and certainly no church home, so that peace quickly evaporated into loss, confusion, and frustration.

Even though I had learned some about Christ, I hadn't really learned much about Satan. I was woefully unprepared for the years of wandering I was about to enter.

But for the first time, I was really beginning to understand Jesus Christ. I was beginning to understand that it wasn't my goodness that determined my ultimate destiny, but my belief on what Jesus accomplished on my behalf because I, like every other human, lacked the necessary goodness.

I also discovered two other crucial things: significance and relevance.

I felt significant to Christ, and I felt significant in Christ. I could sense very strongly that I mattered to Him, I wasn't just a number or some sort of salvation merit badge or notch in a "look-at-how-many-people-I've-brought-to-Christ" gun belt. I mattered, I was important, I was significant. I really had nothing to offer (or so I thought then until He showed me later in life that we all have a purpose), I wasn't rich, or talented or a genius. I was just a plain old mid-seventies dude. I had pimples, a cracking voice and no awards or medals to my name. Yet, I mattered to Him. He cared for me.

And even though I didn't have the grounding in the Bible nor a church home when I returned to Salem, I did have a lasting memory of His peace in my soul and a lasting memory of how true spirit-filled people lived their lives. For you see, I had a seed planted in Malibu that grew into a harvest of understanding that being a Christian was not a title, a thing to do, or even a place to be. It was a lifestyle, it was a genuine adoption and manifestation of Jesus Christ in everything you did; in other words, genuine Christianity was not faked nor filled with hypocrisy. It was a real condition of the heart, a condition that led one to compassion, acceptance and love. I was really beginning to learn what Jesus was referring to when he so often called the religious leaders hypocrites while embracing the baser elements of culture —the hypocrites were in it for nothing more than vain glory— they were posers, fakers, and evil people leading the innocent and ignorant astray. These are the people giving Christianity a bad name. They may be in our pews or even our pulpits; but led to its extreme, these are also the people who go off into their own orbits and form their own systems, systems we call cults.

CHAPTER FIVE

The Lost Years

—+—

"My people are destroyed from lack of knowledge."
—*Hosea, 4:6*

Much is said in the Bible about the wilderness, usually it isn't that pleasant of a place —it's not a crystal clear night in the Wallowa Mountains or a new snow in the Rockies. Instead, often times it's a place of banishment, punishment, flight or severe suffering. Sometimes, however, like with the Apostle Paul, it's a place to find God, a place to learn and grow in the Spirit. He was sent to a desert and spent time in solitude and seeking the Lord —then look what he did! In fact, many prominent Bible figures spent times in some sort of wilderness solitude whether in a cave, or a jail, or hiding by a brook. So wilderness or deserts or retreats aren't always bad. All we have to do is look at the lives of Moses, King David, Joseph, or Elijah to see that. And of course, there's Jesus Himself in the wilderness for 40 days. But it takes maturity and discernment to figure out what sort of wilderness you're in. Have you lost your way out of ignorance or disobedience? Are you finding yourself parched and isolated, frustrated and angry? Or has the Holy Spirit taken you to the wilderness to experience God, to build your dependence on Him and Him alone?

In other words, are you reaping a harvest based upon what you've already sown? Have you made poor decisions or burned bridges in relationships that have now resulted in you being alone? Have you been hurt by others and allowed yourself to grow angry and bitter? Or are you seeking the Lord and asking Him to work in your heart but you're having trouble hearing His voice? Could He be taking you to a place where you'll hear Him better? Maybe there's some trouble you need to learn from or He's asking you to be alone with Him for a while, alone with Him in prayer and digging deeper into His Word.

Once you figure out what sort of wilderness you're in, you can plan your way out accordingly, or, better yet, let God, by His Holy Spirit, guide you around in the wilderness and then eventually out of it. God will always have a purpose for the wilderness, but do we have eyes and ears to see and hear it? Are we interested in His purpose for the wilderness or just trying to get the heck out as soon as possible? Do we lean into the Holy Spirit for guidance and follow where He leads or do we cry out for it to end quickly so we can rush back to our ever-so-comfortable lives? Do we purposely by-pass His learning to return to our conveniences? Is our ease and comfort a higher priority than knowing He Who authors life? Sometimes, however, when our comfortable lives lack His presence our comfort is superficial and is soon shaken off its foundations when the next wilderness rolls around —and they will roll around, if not leap right out at you.

If you are in the wilderness and can't figure out why, you may lack maturity, the seasoning that comes with the Christian journey. If this is your spot, then humility would be a core character trait for what God is up to in your life.

It takes humility to ask for assistance as life's course gets muddy (I've often said life is muddy at it's clearest).

Have you ever asked yourself "why does the proverbial lost male refuse to ask for directions or allow his wife to handle navigating the road map?" Lack of humility. "I'll figure it out myself," he says. Davy Crockett never asked for directions. Neither did Daniel Boone, so I don't need to either. Frankly, how do we know they never did? Most likely they were as successful as they were because at least at some part they were humble enough to seek and take advice, hence, ask for directions. And besides, we need to be pioneers more of the soul than of the terrain. So, humility is really in short supply in our culture —especially if you have a road map and gas station attendant handy to help out but refuse to utilize them, sort of like not reading the Bible or not praying with heart or not talking to that strong Christian friend you know. I believe it is always good advice that when in doubt, ask, whether you're lost in the car or lost in the soul. You may be momentarily embarrassed, but that sure beats a lifetime of suffering after running your hard head into so many brick walls over the years. Momentary embarrassment is a lot better than harvesting a crop of continual sorrow for years of poor choices, and quite possibly even for generations.

Anyway, the trouble for me came in not even recognizing I was in a wilderness. Imagine that. I was wandering around in the suburban desert and didn't even know it! Since I had already unfairly rejected the church, I didn't have the grounding of knowledge of what came next in my young Christian walk. And since I had rejected the church, I didn't know I was lost, that I was in the vast wilderness of postmodern culture, prime prey for the devil and his twists and turns of God's truth. And without being connected to a strong church, I had no one in my life to offer me correction or help. I was alone and wandering around without a map or compass. And the few companions from whom I did occasionally ask for guidance, wound up being as lost as I was. What did Jesus say about the blind leading the blind? Both fall in the ditch, and the ditches of life are usually deep and hard to get out of.

While I love my family, at that time, they were more agnostic than anything so there was not much help in my home with my "God questions". And I didn't know that the youth ministry that had made such a positive impact on me had a branch in my own hometown — if only I had known! But then again, in God's sovereignty, perhaps this all served a purpose.

Ah, but the Bible says in many places, including Romans 10:11 there is no shame in Him. Can you believe that? I need to spend a few words here for God has removed my shame of being in the wilderness for so many years, as well as the shame that came with being a less than adequate spiritual guardian of my home in my first marriage. Sure, I thought I was living for the true God, but as you'll see, I was sorely mistaken. And, yes, my family and I have reaped serious consequences for my poor decisions while in the wilderness, but by the blood of the Lamb, I've been made righteous in Him, justified by His works (see I Corinthians 5:21 and Romans 3:24). I don't have to hang my head low and continually mumble feeble confessions about my past. Instead, I know I am saved and one of His children now and for eternity (Romans 8:15-17 and 10:9-13). In fact, I can even proclaim His glory and His salvation, instead of being timid and quiet. I can live out loud for His calling on my life, I can live out loud for Jesus Christ! (See Matthew 28:19-20 and II Thessalonians 1:11.)

Well, back to our regular programming.

Once home I didn't know what to do with my newfound faith in Jesus Christ. So the further I got from that wonderful week, the more anemic my faith became and the more susceptible I was to what ever wind of doctrine came blowing my way.

While my high school years were pretty tame in my faith delusion, my college years were not. High school softened me up for the big blows that came later. I had a lot of "churchy" or "religiousy" friends, but they didn't really exude the joy I would have expected. They also didn't exhibit the disciplined life I thought true Christians would have. They didn't talk about the Bible, they never mentioned what Jesus had done or was doing for them, and I never saw them pray. In other words, they were more closet Christians, seemingly satisfied with keeping their faith on the shelf unless at church on Sunday or they were being watched by their pastor.

College, however, was filled with searing liberalism, active atheists, regional religions, and a strong anti-Christian flavor. The university I went to certainly was no paragon of conservatism, much less an institution that embraced anything Christlike. I was clueless to the fact I was in a spiritual wasteland, a dark pit or trap laid so secretly for our young and impressionable learners and shapers of the future. Anti-Christian discussions were fostered and even touted as being quite intellectual, but any discussion about Christ was seen as backwards and old-fashioned. So, in challenging my own faith, I was supposedly exercising and strengthening the mind I was paying so dearly to educate. Little did I know, that couched within all that learning and intellectualizing of life, I was also chiseling away at what little foundation I had in Christ.

Drugs and sex were not the lure for me they were for so many others. Instead, I was lured by the many "isms" available on campus: Buddhism, Marxism, relativism, and a host of others leaping out at me daily. My faith was becoming so fragmented and diluted by the post-modern culture that I started thinking that maybe God was an ape. This seemed perfectly logical to me at the time because it would begin to marry together the whole evolution vs. creation debate. I was so caught up in my own intellectualism that I thought I was on to something; a way to hang onto the tattered shreds of my faith without having to denounce any of the education I was receiving. I could even see myself on "Nightline" talking about this incredible breakthrough discovery, and Ted Koppel would be asking "why hasn't anyone ever thought of this before?"

While you may laugh at this now, I was really serious about this line of thought. I was so theologically and scientifically ignorant, I thought I was smart. (At the end of this work is a list of many resources you can read and study to better prepare yourself and your children for similar debates you're sure to run into — true science will always corroborate God, not refute Him, Intelligent Design is being more and more supported by scientific fact but more and more shunned and resisted by that same scientific community — especially as it relates to public educations.)

The few Bible studies I did attend had no meat to them so radical liberalism and anemic Christianity were continually shaking my faith. The worst part of this was totally losing grasp of who and what Jesus Christ was and is. In college, the closest I got to an understanding of Jesus Christ was while I was working at a local NBC affiliate TV station. During one week, as I was preparing for the 11 o'clock nightly news, I caught snippets of *Jesus of Nazareth* each night throughout the week. It wasn't too graphic and what I did catch of it I enjoyed, and some segments even caused me to deeply reflect what little I knew of my faith. But I particularly enjoyed the portrayal of Jesus as being intelligent and peaceful, but that He also exhibited courage and compassion.

But sad to say, that was about all of Jesus I got in college —and I would be misguided about Jesus for many years to come.

Chapter Six

Who's the Potter,
Who's the Pot?

———+———

"But who are you, O man, to talk back to God?
—*Romans 9:20*

C an you explain the Trinity? Probably not. Do you know anyone who can explain it really well? Probably not. Why?

This little discourse deceives more lives than we'll ever know, mine included. But some understanding of the Trinity is absolutely vital to grasping the deeper concepts of Christianity and is equally vital to protecting yourself from the whims and wills of cults or other anti-Christian organizations. Yet as simple as the Trinity may seem, it is one of the most difficult concepts for our minds to grasp — how can one Entity express Himself in three different ways without losing His oneness or His central identity?

As you might imagine, the answer isn't easy, but we need some baseline of understanding as we move through the remainder of this work; and, we will also need some small doses of faith as well.

Perhaps that f-word, "faith", throws you a bit. Well, are you breathing right now? Of course you are. Do you see the air you're breathing? The answer is no. Oh, I know, in some really polluted areas we see the smog and comment how dirty the air is, or if it's cold we see steam coming from our mouths, but neither of these are air. They are only manifestations or evidences that air exists. Air in itself is an invisible gas: oxygen. We see evidences of its movements, but we don't see air itself, but you still breathe because you believe, thus, have faith, that air exists.

Another example would be the proverbial example of a car. In the morning as you awake and go about your routine of readying for work, the last thing on your mind is probably your car. But still, you hop into it and put the key into the ignition with the full expectation it'll start. You have faith that you have gas and the right key. But a deeper example of this is you trust the engine runs. You probably never met the folks who built the car, or the designers of the car or even the driver who shipped it to your dealership. But there you are, sitting in the driver's seat ready to start the engine of the car you know so little about. Think about it. If you're not a mechanic, you probably can't explain the details of the brakes or the carburetor or even the distributor cap. In fact, you can't even see them but you "know" they're there —so in you go, plopping down in that upholstered seat expecting it to start at the slightest twist of a small, carved piece of metal.

These are simple definitions of faith —believing when you don't see or even fully understand. We don't see God, but we see evidences of His existence all over, the earth being one example. (I know hard-core atheists and evolutionists would disagree. Again, at the end of this book is a short list or resources to assist you with the creation/evolution debate, but as a teaser, more and more scientific evidence clearly points in the direction of Intelligent design. In fact, it takes more faith to be an atheist because of all the mounting evidence proving God's existence.)

A couple of last points on faith.

Jesus states that God is Spirit (John 4:24). Prior to this, Jesus is talking to Nicodemus about being "born from above" ("born again" in other vernaculars). In this discourse He explains to Nicodemus that the spirit is like the wind: "The wind blows wherever it pleases. You hear its sound, but you cannot tell where it comes from or where it is going" (John 3:8). What is wind but moving air? So it is with the spirit, it is real, but we can't see it. Truthfully speaking, the spirit is a He.

Now that we've discussed a little bit about faith, let's return to the subject of the Trinity.

I remember watching a movie, *Nuns on the Run* I think it was called. It had a couple of the comics from Great Britain's Monty Python's Flying Circus in it. The movie itself was funny; and as I recall the basic premise, the two main characters (the Monty Python comics) were trying to flee the mob so they disguised themselves as nuns and took haven in a convent. Imagine these two characters, two hardened bad guys (and really funny comics), pretending to be nuns. It was a great formula for a comedy. Well, one scene has one of the men (Eric Aidel is the comic's real name) dressed as a nun teaching a classroom full of uniformed little kids. One of the kids asks the inevitable question: "Sister so-and-so, just what is the Trinity?"

With the appropriate hemming and hawing of a criminal pretending to be a nun, he simply said, "well, it's like a three-leaf clover. Each leaf is equal but yet separate."

The child responds with something like, "I still don't understand."

More hemming and hawing ensues and then, mercifully, the bell rings and all the kids flee the classroom to lunch or recess. And the "teacher" breathes a long sigh of relief!

This seemingly harmless, yet funny, dialogue is sadly a great example of how most people address the Trinity. While I'm no theological expert, I can certainly tell you the damage that happens if you have no understanding of the Trinity. Even a minor or basic knowledge will suffice to save you from years of groping about for deeper understanding of God's identity. Not having a basic understanding of the Trinity, or rejecting the concept altogether, stands you directly in the path of any number of devilishly conceived and sublimely disguised counterfeits —none of which will lead you to a true understanding of Jesus Christ, which then, will leave you blind to the significance of His sacrifice on the Cross on the hill of Golgotha.

My first insight in this area is one of pride. How dare we, the created, explain the Creator?

It reminds me of the crew in Roman 1:18-32. These folks became so conceited in themselves that they started to worship the creation rather than the creator. They were worshipping themselves, their bodies, and graven images they carved themselves. This self-worship lead to all kinds of evil, including personal debauchery and spiritual destruction. They were so hardened in their hearts that they continually defied the Living God to the point where He allowed them to continue in their abject sin. God went so far as to call these people "God-haters" (v. 30). Not company I want to be in.

Yet, what was at the core of their God-hating? The same thing at the core of Lucifer's rebellion: pride. Lucifer started off as the Angel of Light. He was beautiful and was compared to many precious gems (see Isaiah 14:12-19[1] and Ezekiel 28:13-19). But he started thinking to himself that "I will be like the most high." He wanted to be the top dog and started to marshal his way to do so. Such activity, understandably, got him kicked out of Heaven, he and those who supported him were banished forever from Heaven.

So the sin of pride is not a new one, and it's not just our own pride that grips us in trickery. In fact, I believe it is the trap we unknowingly fall into. Our pride, or getting caught up in someone else's pride, sets us to thinking that not only can we explain God, but after a while, we don't even need God. Or, what happens more often than not, is that God is defined in a man-made way, stuffed in a little man-made construction and placed out of sight. That way, the man-made god can then be used as a fear motivator rather than as the Author of love and the Bringer of Salvation.

Again, I believe this is the basic premise of cults and why they so distort the Trinity and the incarnate identity of Jesus Christ. They want to remove Him from deity and place themselves there. If you remove the One Who actually deserves, yes, has even earned our worship, then anything, or anyone, can take His place if we allow it.

Sounds horrific doesn't it? Yet we see it all the time.

But why is it so many of us fall for such a devastating trap?

CHAPTER SEVEN

Who Is This Jesus?

————+————

"In God's dimension...you find a being who is three persons while remaining one being."
                    —C.S. Lewis, Mere Christianity

I think very few, if any, of us start our search for God by thinking, "I want to become God." Rather, we usually begin with a vague curiosity of origin, origin of humanity, origin of earth, or just plain old origin of life.

The question of origin is itself a very weighty question to ask. It requires grappling with science, religion, the way we were raised, hence psychology, and a whole host of other variables. Again, the end of this book has a list of resources to assist with these questions.

For this discussion, however, I will simply assume we agree there is a God, or at least we are willing to consider there is a God, and we're wondering how to get to Him. How do we discover or even encounter God? In this wonder, we are considering the God of the Holy Bible; the Christian God Who was most expressly manifested in the Person of Jesus

Christ and through His written Word, what we refer to as the Holy Bible.

Foundationally, from a Christian perspective, we are to hold the Word of God to a very high degree because it originated from Him and not from a bunch of men collaborating over the years. While men indeed were responsible to "pen", or dictate, the Scripture, the Scripture says of Itself it is "God-breathed" (2 Timothy 3:16); that It came "not from men's minds, but from men as they were inspired and led by the Holy Spirit" (2 Peter 1:20-21); and that God has "exalted His Word above all things along with His name" (Psalm 138:2b). Because our culture holds itself in such high esteem, it is difficult to grasp the idea that a written document could originate from any source other than us. History is built on the writings of people and civilizations. Whether on paper or etched in stone, mankind has been documenting itself in one form or another since its beginning.

But if we have just an inkling of belief that God is the creator of this vast and apparently infinite universe, then why is it such a stretch to think that the God who cast the galaxies across the inky blackness could not or would not initiate a Holy Writ for our consideration? In other words, God has not left us deaf, dumb, and blind about His creation nor about the inner depths of His heart, for that is what the Bible reveals — His heart toward us, His creation.

This said, then we need to grapple with just who was Jesus Christ and why are we so easily swayed from what the Bible teaches about Him. Some say He was a great man, or a great teacher, or a great prophet. Yet the Bible seems to say, that while He was all these things and more, He was also God in the flesh (many of the resources have exhaustive lists of Scriptural references to Christ's deity). While there are a lot of references regarding Christ's deity, there are three I would like to mention here because of their clarity and their personal impact on my life.

Going in order, the first reference is John 8:57-59:

"You are not yet fifty years old," the Jews said to him, "and you have seen Abraham?"

"I tell you the truth," Jesus answered, "before Abraham was born, *I am!*"

At this they picked up stones to stone him, but Jesus hid himself. (Emphasis added.)

What is the significance of the phrase "I am?" Couldn't He have just as easily said "I was?" The simple answer is yes, He could have said "I was," but that would have implied different things than "I Am." For instance, the word "was" implies something different from the past, or something that once was has now ended. The term "I am" clearly speaks to pre-existence. Jesus Christ was every bit as alive before Abraham's time as He is to the Jew who is asking this question.

"I Am" also implies significant biblical aspects. In Exodus 3:1-15, beginning in verse one, God appears to Moses in a burning bush and informs him he will be sent back to the people of Israel and to the Pharaoh himself, to proclaim freedom for the Israelite nation. Just think of it! You're minding your own business, performing your work duties of tending the flock of sheep belonging to your father-in-law (nice of him to give you a job), when all of the sudden the Angel of the Lord appears in this bush by way of fire. Not only that, but the bush is not being burned up, and out of the midst of the burning bush you hear your name being called. Moses is at the most significant crossroads of his life. Will he obey God? Or will he shrink away from the call God is clearly and phenomenally placing on his life? Thankfully, he accepts this enormous call to serve God as the instrument of deliverance for his people. So he started his day a simple shepherd, and he concluded it as God's anointed leader. Now that's a big day!

But before this extremely unusual encounter is over, he asks God, "Who should I say sent me?" Instead of waiting for an answer, he suggests how about "the God of your fathers has sent me to you, and they ask me 'What is his name?' Then what shall I tell them?" God could have said, "the Great God of the Universe," or "the Almighty Sovereign Lord Over Everything," but He didn't, he said "I AM who I AM is what you are to say to the Israelites: I AM has sent me to you." I AM is what God says is His name and that has always been His name and always will be His name.

Now fast forward to Jesus calling Himself I Am. In fact, He calls Himself I Am several times in the Gospels. All of these take on the same connotation of God, Yahweh, calling Himself I Am. So the implication is clear— Jesus Christ is proclaiming Himself to be the God of Abraham. Under Hebrew law at the time, for a person to do this was blasphemy, punishable by death. That is why they picked up stones to kill Him—because He used the same phrase God applies to Himself. In other words, He just called Himself God in the flesh.

While the implication of Jesus referring to Himself as I Am didn't escape the people of that culture, it sure has escaped us in our culture.

Another key Scripture is found in John 17:5 where Jesus is praying aloud for Himself while His disciples are present:

"And now, Father, glorify me in your presence with the glory I had with you before the world began."

This verse rings so loudly about Jesus' pre-existence it's not even funny. Yet it has been overlooked by so many all these years. And the people who establish cults or other counter-religions sure don't want to bring this to your attention. Yet, there it sits, in all its clearness, smack-dab in the middle of the Gospel of John.

This is a great verse to explore word by word with a good concordance. But I'll touch on a few key points. The whole verse is about a past-tense experience Jesus actually had. Some people teach that this was solely in God's foreknowledge, meaning, it didn't actually happen, it was just something

God foresaw as happening at some future point. However, the grammatical construction does not lead to this conclusion at all. For one thing, if that were true, then Jesus Himself would have no knowledge of this experience, thus, no recollection of the glory referred to because He wasn't there. It would be nothing more than a future expectation of God's rather than a direct experience of Jesus', so Jesus would not be able to refer to an experience He had not actually had yet. Plus the context with the word 'presence' clearly refers to a shared experience —Jesus and God, and presumably the Holy Spirit are together in community in this experience (Jesus is praying by way of the Spirit so His involvement is automatic).

The word 'world' is also rendered 'ages', 'universe', or even 'creation' in other reliable texts. Therefore, the experience Jesus is referring to began even before creation began (a companion verse to this is Colossians 1:17 where it states "He is before all things"). This indicates Jesus was in existence before creation, before mankind, and even before any consciousness other than that of the triune God even existed.

The third reference is Philippians 2:5-11. This particular section takes on two key concepts: the deity of Christ, and His humility to shed Himself of His deity so that He could be the once and for all sacrifice for mankind (see Hebrews 10:14). Verses six and seven of Philippians 2 are our main focus:

"Who [Christ], being in the very nature God, did not consider equality with God something to be grasped, but made Himself nothing, taking the very nature of a servant, being made in human likeness."

I used to think this verse meant that Jesus was only being compared to God instead of Him being God Incarnate. But what difference does it make either way?

Quite a lot actually. Just think if you or I were the Creator, would we be willing to come and dwell among the very people who blaspheme and ridicule us? Or would we get even then and there, giving them no chance for redemption? Thankfully, unlike us, He chose redemption. Not just any redemption, but the eternal redemption of mankind by becoming one of us and dwelling among us. He demonstrated the ultimate humility that when He could lift a finger and wipe everything out, He instead brought love, light, peace, and grace, so disturbing the religious establishment of that time they had Him crucified. Imagine, the Creator of the universe being nailed to the Cross on our behalf, and not only that, the community of God the Father, God the Son, and God the Holy Spirit being separated for the first time. However brief the separation was, it was intense enough for Him to bear the stipulation of carrying the sins of the whole world!

Jesus didn't come to redeem just mankind, He also is the redeemer and the restorer of the Earth, for there will one day be a new Heaven and a New Earth (see Revelation 21)!

Here's another thought I'd like to share. One recent stormy Tuesday, December night, I had finished a message at the local rescue mission about Jesus from the birth to the Cross. My premise was while the birth was indeed miraculous, its full miraculous impact culminated on the Cross upon which Jesus gave His life for you and me. Afterward, men in various trials of life huddled around asking for prayer, or asking questions, or just hanging around —what a great privilege to extol Jesus to a receptive crowd of seekers! One gentleman timidly approached me as the remaining crowd dispersed to the dinner line. He asked me one simple but very complex question I had never been asked before: "if God created the universe, where did God come from?"

A question many have asked for centuries, but never to me.

Taking a deep breath with a heart prayer for the Holy Spirit to guide me, I began to answer him. "It is very difficult for our finite minds to grasp something that is infinite. Our minds are more accustomed to understanding the here and now, or at least the tangible and concrete. When things begin to get into areas we're uncomfortable with, concepts like 'forever' or 'always', we struggle with them." Here I paused and again quickly prayed that I was on, or at least, near the mark that the Holy Spirit was leading me to. Then I continued.

"In the Bible God states that He wills that all men be saved and come into the knowledge of the truth. So God is desiring for us to know things, to grasp and understand knowledge, but He also calls us at times to have faith, to believe in something He states that we either can't see for ourselves, like the Holy Spirit, or things we struggle to comprehend, like God has always been and always will be." Then the thought for this chapter hit me!

"But God knowing how our minds would struggle with this, chose to come to His people in the flesh in Jesus Christ. Yes, He came in the flesh to basically redeem mankind, but don't you also think He came in the flesh because we might better grasp Who and What He is when we see a beginning with His birth and an end with His crucifixion?" He seemed to accept the explanation and both of us were walking away shaking our heads.

But could that be another reason God came in the flesh? Is it so far out to think that God so loves us that He packaged Himself into a finite bundle we could see, hear, touch, and follow? I realize there are more spiritually significant reasons for Him coming in the flesh, but this just seems like another bonus God gives us at no extra charge. It's just one more example of the extremes God goes to get our attention, to get us to turn aside and look long enough to see Him, to ponder Him, and to ponder our lives in relation to Him.

As we close this chapter, we also must admit that we are in a lousy position to explain God. We must accept when God says "For my thoughts are not your thoughts, neither are your ways my ways, declares the Lord" (Isaiah 55:8). How many inventions do we see explaining the inventors? The Model

T never explained Henry Ford nor did penicillin explain Luis Pastor. Moonlit Sonata didn't explain Beethoven nor did Snoopy ever explain Charles Shultz. So too, then, is the question of how can we the created fully explain the Creator? Bottom line is we can't. We can only attempt to make sense of the clues He's given us, and two of the biggest clues are found in the person of Jesus Christ and the Word of God, the Holy Bible.

Other than seeing God in Creation, there is no way for Him to communicate with us other than becoming a man —invading planet earth and specifically speaking to us in a language we can understand. Imagine that you're looking at an anthill and bearing down on the anthill is a giant bulldozer, poised to wipe it out of existence. The ants are so busy going about their bustling lives that they pay no notice to the distant rumbling. You desperately yell at them to inform them of their pending doom but to no avail, they don't even acknowledge you. The only solution is for you to become an ant and warn them face to face in their own language. God did just that in the person of Jesus Christ.

The question is, are we listening?

CHAPTER EIGHT

The Snare of Self —
The Desire to Belong

———+———

"The self-conscious human individual, then, takes or assumes the organized social attitudes of the given social group...to which he belongs."
— *George Herbert Mead, Mind, Self, & Society.*

"Let this mind be in you which was also in Christ Jesus."
— *Philippians 2:5*

The last chapter started with the statement that few if any of us search for God with a desire of becoming God. Then the chapter dove into what the Bible says of Jesus Christ. In Chapter Seven we explored pride. In this chapter I hope to weave the two together with these prevailing concepts:

1). We are schooled to think of ourselves as the primary definers of our realities.

We see it everywhere from personnel issues in the workplace to sociology to anthropology. We see it in the way various "people groups" socialize themselves around common interests (Little League enthusiasts to bar-be-cue enthusiasts to car enthusiasts, and so on). We see it also in the way our culture mass markets consumer goods: we need more stuff to help us become better people, or to become more popular or to just look cool. Or we want to look better so we decide we need to lose weight or have enhancements of some kind to be more acceptable to the people groups we desire to belong to or to look like how we think we're supposed to look. Everything primarily revolves around ourselves and improving ourselves with very little thought of the next guy, much less the next generation. Secondly, our desires revolve around being accepted by others, even if it means becoming something other than ourselves.

2). Cult leaders desperately try to "un-deify" Christ so they can replace Him with themselves and then receive the adoration and worship that rightfully belongs to Jesus. They do this by playing on the above concept where they try to appeal to your ego or pride or insecurity or your desire to just belong to something. But rather than replacing it with high esteem in yourself, or with confidence in Jesus, they replace it with themselves and their desires and demands by minimizing your humanity and Christ's deity. The trade-off for this is you now belong to a people group from whom you can gain personal identity from; therefore, the marginalized and disillusioned of society make attractive targets. However, your "standing" or status in the group, thus your identity in the group, is only as strong as your dedication and compliance with meeting the group's demands and expectations placed on you by its leader, and enforced by his core group of "leaders," or what Dogbert refers to as "enforcers". This is how your humanity is minimized, by slowly being influenced to be a conformer of the group rather than being who God originally designed you to be.

This sounds easy to figure out and avoid, but is it? If it were, why are so many educated and intelligent people parts of large cults throughout the world? It's astounding to think of all the people who flock to the various buildings, temples, shrines, classes and seminars to worship an organization constructed by a man for his own benefit, not their benefit; and certainly not for God's benefit.

But flock people do.

We so desperately desire a sense of belonging that we may very well ignore the still small voice in the back of our minds warning us to be wary, and instead dive head long into a group that seems to desire us as much as we desire to belong, to feel needed, and, yes, to feel worthy. Thus, we now belong to a group of people who are as insecure, or more so than ourselves, so we're all waiting for some sort of direction for us to unite around to further solidify our collective identity, to give us something that we can say, "yes, this is my team and I am an integral member of it!" This then sets the stage for the overall leader to step in with his winning words of acceptance and inspiration but with very subtle and evil undertones of oppression lurking between each sentence uttered or written. Ever so slowly they begin to carefully instill their desires and philosophies in ways that may be veiled from the masses that just want to belong and connect. Our over-riding desire of acceptance drowns out the clarion sirens of caution as we willingly and excitedly consider, and eventually embrace, what they are saying.

So the indoctrination begins with classes, seminars, and various writings of subtle but shocking subject matter.

Take for example one of the main texts of the group of which I was a part. This text is called *Jesus Christ is Not God*. The text is steeped in what appears to be sound logic and educated conclusions and research. Some quotes from this book include:

"...I am saying that Jesus Christ is not God, but the Son of God" (p. 5).

"Jesus Christ was not and is not God; neither are we" (p. 57).

"It [his previous discussion points] has already been established that Jesus and God are not one from the beginning" (p. 121)[2].

While the "arguments" put forth in this writing seem convincing and the author's apparent "knowledge" of language may seem extensive, he actually has many flaws of understanding, comes to illogical conclusions on theology, and he often misrepresents actual historical figures and events[3]. Plus, he inserts and deletes words from the biblical text because, according to him, his changes better explain God's intent. In reality he's subtly changing the meaning of the passage quoted. But of course, he never mentions this and if the reader doesn't know where or how to verify his "information", the reader may very well receive the information as truthful and accurate since it's presented in no-nonsense, authoritative language. Also since he's the leader of this group, we now have a strong sense of belonging along with a burgeoning friendship base. Thus, the author is playing on the dulling of the warning signals and the expectation that the masquerade of his research will bluff the reader into believing the author's credentials are honest and the text is true.

And oddly enough, this author indicates he has a Ph. D., yet there is no record of him ever being enrolled in the very institution from which he claims to have received his doctorate. Therefore, it is always wise to keep in the back of our minds that people aren't always as they portray themselves!

Please keep in mind that I've only provided a very small percentage of evidence from the group of which I was a part, and also keep in mind this group is one of many throughout the world attempting to "un-deify" Jesus Christ, they insert their own philosophies and opinions, which are basically flimsy attempts to hide their original intent of exalting themselves to a position of receiving your adoration and worship, and, of course, your money.

On the lighter side, this reminds me of quotes from Dilbert where the dog character, Dogbert, tells his owner, Dilbert, "I'm going to form a personality cult to honor me, I'll take all their money and make them wear bathrobes with my picture on the back." Except for the bathrobe part, this rings eerily true!

Another note of caution is often that once legitimate churches are nothing more than a reflection of the presiding pastor or the chair of the elder board or the congregation's largest donor, thus, they maintain the façade of a church when they're really nothing more than a group of people being led by a personality bent on power rather than by Jesus. Sounds a lot like a cult to me! And, ironically, this is what turned me off to churches in the first place, and I still wound up in a cult —go figure. So, as you seek churches, be sure you're really listening to where God is leading you and also really scrutinize what they say they believe compared to what they actually teach —you may be quite surprised.

As an example, new neighbors of ours, a Christian family moving from Omaha to Salem, were looking for churches to join. They went to one large local church where the pastor preached on Easter about the importance of teaching our children the true meaning of Easter rather than being focused on nothing but candy. He emphasized a focus on the risen Christ and not chocolate bunnies. Sounded like a good sermon until they went to pick up their kids at the children's ministry area. When they asked their kids what they learned about Jesus and the resurrection, the kids said they learned nothing. Instead they just looked for and ate candy, particularly chocolate bunnies. Needless to say, they never returned to that church. Why?

Because they weren't unified as a bible-believing, God-honoring church. Rather, they were a bunch of little fiefdoms and egos jockeying for prominence within the congregation. Sadly it's a common occurrence in today's church: what comes out of the pulpit and what is actually practiced are opposites, thus, hypocrisy is the atmosphere produced and the air being breathed. In other words, many churches are nothing more than turf battles rather than beacons for the kingdom of God.

So, just because there's a church and someone's called a pastor, is no guarantee at all that they're genuine —structures and titles mean nothing, God looks on the heart, so it is the motive of the heart that speaks loudly. Strive to seek out their motives, ask questions, read their documents, and even attend leaders meetings whether you're invited or not: If they balk at any of these, they most likely have something they're hiding, and that isn't a godly church. (Some issues need to be confidential, but those are usually the exception rather than the norm. If a church insists everything is confidential, then suspicion is rightfully aroused.)

While the last few paragraphs may seem a digression, they're intentional because it is often those kinds of less-than-genuine church experiences that cause many people to lose trust in churches and thus become susceptible to either rejecting Christianity altogether, or to be vulnerable to so-called non-church Christian groups. And you can certainly bet that cult leaders know people are turned off by the churches and therefore position themselves as the genuine article of Christianity whereas the churches are nothing but counterfeits to what God originally intended. In other words, cults will prey on the many anemic churches dotting our country, pointing to these churches as representative of all churches, thus, all churches are to be avoided; this creates the void the cults can then fill.

CHAPTER NINE

Messages, Meaning, and Tactics

—✝—

"Word": Gk, eirein, to say, to speak; a) something that is said; b) talk, discourse.
—Webster's New Collegiate Dictionary, 1981.

"Word": Gk, logos, a saying or statement by God.
—Vine's Complete Expository Dictionary, 1996.

"In our ordinary language we often use one word to refer to many unique objects in many different settings..."
—F. J. Roethlisberger, Of Words and Men.

*) *n reading the Bible, the word 'church' is the Greek word *'ecclesia'*. This word basically means a group of people called out for a common purpose (you can double-check this definition in any reputable concordance or Bible dictionary). For instance, a group of people meeting to discuss a civil matter would meet this definition, so would people gathering

to worship a common god. The key points in this definition are not hinged on one theme or type of meeting, or on a building or specific structure. In other words, the term church is related to people with a common purpose or pursuit, and not to a place or a building. Yet Jesus clearly said He would "build His church..." (Matthew 16:18). So what was Jesus referring to and why is it important to this discussion?

Two reasons.

First, we must endeavor to understand just what our Lord and Savior was referring to so we can be sure that whatever we do or where ever we go, abides within His original vision and design for accessing and worshipping Him. Are our pursuits really within His call upon our lives or are we merely following after a man-made construct of traditional ritual, familiarity or comfort?

Secondly, my experiences with cults indicate they really try to convince people that 'church' wasn't a congregation of people or a structure, which is technically true; therefore, the practicing 'church' as an organized group in a specific structure was not what Jesus intended so it should be shunned and a new model should be adopted; the model, of course, put forth by the cult. This has an interesting irony because most cults are more organized than any church ever hoped to be! But more on that later.

But this thinking just on its own doesn't make sense. Where ever Jesus went big crowds gathered, often following him for miles until He settled down to rest or eat. Why did the crowds come? Did they have a primary purpose in pursuing Jesus, or were they all just hanging around the same place or traveling the same roads at the same time? Of course not. They all gathered for the express purpose of seeing Jesus and hearing Him preach and teach the Word of God. So guess what He did? He preached and taught the Word of God. Therefore, the gathering being there for one purpose —to see and hear Jesus —was technically an *ecclesia*, a church, and Jesus acknowledged and honored the gathering by teaching and preaching. And sometimes there were even miracles performed. If the church was such a sin, why did Jesus Himself give it such respect, and even encourage it? He obviously didn't have trouble rebuking the forces of darkness— confronting the Pharisees and turning over the money-changer tables —yet He allows these gatherings to occur and, in fact, gives them credence by addressing them and even at times healing them. There was no rebuking on His part, only allowance and, to some degree, reverence —seeing the masses so desperately seeking after God moved His heart.

What's more, Jesus went to into the temple to preach and teach. He knew there would be people there for the sole purpose of worshipping God. Thus, the Jewish temple was definitely the precursor for the modern church as a structure and gathering place for seeking the Lord.

So, what was Jesus referring to when He mentioned 'church'?

I'm no theologian but I agree with the vast majority of them when they indicate the 'church' was taking on a whole new aspect. By studying the context of the term 'church' and watching how the first century church developed in the Book of Acts and throughout the New Testament, it's clear that church was a much more encompassing concept than just a gathering. It was meant to be a living body, an organism, unified together in Christ (see Ephesians 3:3-6) and cemented through the working of the Holy Spirit (I Corinthians 12:13). The church was to become a body spanning the globe as more and more people accepted Christ as Savior and Lord, but for this body to be continually fed and able to grow, it had to have smaller units of gathering. These units would eventually make up what we commonly think of as churches, or church buildings. In fact, in the New Testament there are many references to larger assemblies, hence, churches; and then references to smaller gatherings in people's homes. (There are many references through the New Testament, here are just a few: Acts 20:20, 28; I Corinthians 1:2; Galatians 1:13; I Thessalonians 1:1; II Thessalonians 1:1; and I Timothy 3:5.)

But why do the cults apparently disregard so many clear scriptural references to the proper building of a church?

To answer this we return to the topic of Chapter Seven, *Who is this Jesus?* We established there that cults "undeify" Jesus Christ. They say He is not God and then they minimize all references to His deity. They go to such lengths that many cults will spend a lot of time in the Old Testament with little time in the New Testament and virtually no time at all in the Gospels. Why? Because the gospels clearly indicate Christ's authority, His love, and His deity (who else was the Word in the flesh, who else can walk on water, cause the blind to see or the deaf to hear, or turn ordinary water into the finest quality wine?).

Bluntly stated, cults promulgate a doctrine that can only be explained as anti-Christ. To reduce Christ's rightful position as Head, is nothing short of blasphemous and is of itself a doctrine of devils. But people keep believing it and once cults are able to keep people from seeing the supreme significance of Christ, they can instead slip in their own doctrine peppered with a few verses of scripture and then say their teaching is the truth. As an example, the leader of the cult I was in was so adamant about Jesus not being God, that he added 44 words to John 1:1-14, the passage of Scripture stating Jesus was the Word and the Word was God[4]. And this wasn't the only instance this author added (or subtracted) from very clear scripture references on Jesus Christ's deity. But so long as adoration was going to Christ, it wasn't going to him, so he had to put a stop to it by cleverly casting himself as a biblical expert, and then went about surgically removing clear references to Christ's deity. Once he had Christ stripped down to a mere man, then he, a mere man, could insert his own authority over the church he was forming. In other words, he bumped off the leader and assumed the position himself.

This particular behavior is almost universal among cults.

One very large cult believes that Jesus was once imperfect and came about from a male earth god having sexual inter-course with his celestial wife[5]. Yet another prominent cult teaches Jesus was an angel existing in three different phases[6]. What's really frightening is these last two groups are very prominent in this country, and have vast numbers in member-ship, and many high-ranking and influential public officials who make and interpret laws locally and nationally are deeply involved in these cults.

So, given all this, cults have to deny the scriptural basis for church because it is to be founded on Christ and Christ alone. Anything else would be a man-made construct, or as the prophet Jeremiah said of men rejecting God to form their own beliefs: "my people have done two evil things: They have forsaken me — the fountain of living water. And they have dug for themselves cracked cisterns that can hold no water at all!" (2:13 NLT.) Other translations call the cisterns "broken", while the Message transla-tion calls them "cisterns that leak, cisterns that are no better than sieves." Without Christ, the Bible simply doesn't make sense, and, without Christ, there is no salvation and there is no church.

Throughout the New Testament we read continual refer-ences to the church being established in Christ. The clearest reference to me is Ephesians Chapter 1. The whole chapter is about how we are adopted through Jesus Christ (verse 5), that heaven and earth will be under Christ (verse 10), that our hope is in Him (verse 12), that we have exerted power in Christ (verses 19-20), and that He is the head of the church, which is His body (verses 22-23).

Colossians 1:15-29 is another clear passage speaking to Christ's deity and supremacy.

In summary, always be wary of any religion that purports the minimization of Christ's deity to then insert their own writings to explain why. If you can't document it in the Book, that is, the Bible, then move on!

Another area of control is in terms of vocabulary. Red flags should quickly pop up when ever a group of people or a specific leader begins taking relatively common words and starts saying they're taboo. Often they will follow their declaration of a word or phrase being taboo with their own definitions or substitute words.

This sounds confusing but let me see if I can explain this by way of two personal examples.

The group I was in really discouraged the use of the term 'create' or 'created'. They contended that "created," meant to bring something into existence out of nothing, and they further contend that only God could do that. Take a moment to briefly explore the subtleties of that last sentence. While their definition is technically correct and they are further technically correct that only God can bring something into existence out of nothing, they are also using only one aspect of the overall definition of the word "created" — it can also mean, among other things, to produce or bring about by a course of action or to produce through imaginative skill[7]. Yet when ever a person in the organization used this term in context of anything other than God, they found themselves severely confronted for using a word that was wrong and then they would be corrected with the right words to say. Right words for replacing the word "created" included "invented" or "developed", both synonyms meaning basically the same thing[8]. More often than not, this whole confrontation took place in front of one's friends and family — thus — the use of this simple word turned into an onslaught of humiliation and embarrassment that was not soon forgotten.

Another example is the term "Christmas". This organization relied upon reputable research in archeology and astronomy demonstrating that Jesus Christ was not born in December, but in September. However, because of this, they banned the use of the term "Christmas" as being pagan and even devilish. Whenever anyone used this word, they would again face the same type of confrontation just described above, and again, this confrontation would also often be public and thus another episode of humiliation and embarrassment. Acceptable substitutes included phrases such as "ho-ho" or "the holidays".

Just think of this, while the rest of the world, strong Christians and non-Christians alike are all using the term "Christmas", there we were using an infantile phrase like "ho-ho". It's laughable now, but then it was isolating.

Which I believe is exactly the point.

Language is symbolic at its very basic form. Letters are symbols strung together to form words and sentences to express thoughts externally to be shared with others. This is the basis for all human communication, both the written and spoken word. Words are so important that God penned His Word, the Bible, in words so it could be passed down through the ages, God didn't put the Bible in pictures or the oral tradition to be passed down through the ages. He had it written. Words, hence language is very important, and language, of course, is what produces communication. That is one reason why the founders of the United States were quite emphatic about maintaining our freedom of speech. Words are power.

However, once these symbolic modes of communication are under control, then communication itself is under control, at least external communication. Once external communication is under control, how much longer is it until internal communication is under control?

What is internal communication? Your thoughts. Stop and think about whom you spend the most time "talking" to. It's yourself. Most likely these thoughts are dominated by words, phrases, sentences and so on. Sure, quite a bit of our thinking is visual, but psychologically we think in a combination of verbal and visual, but which controls which? Often times vocabulary determines the visual in our thinking. In fact, vocabulary, hence language, often defines our perspective of reality, or at least critical aspects of our reality. Cultural anthropologists and cultural communication experts agree: "language participates in our perception and in our expression of perception; we cannot divorce language from perception or thought"[9].

With all of this in mind, we can observe multi-layered tactics of the cult at work. They begin to control aspects of language while at the same time ushering this control, along with humiliation coupled with embarrassment. Pretty soon, if a person chooses to allow this treatment to occur, he finds himself becoming increasingly insecure in himself, which then drives him to seek an even deeper identity in the very group that is fomenting the insecurity.

So what is happening with these seemingly minor language distinctions? It is the breaking of a person's spirit, not the Holy Spirit, but the spark and enthusiasm they have for life. They are slowly losing confidence in their own identity and grasping for the group to fill the draining loss. Thus, the group begins to form its own micro-culture with its own twists of language, which then control, to a degree anyway, the thinking of its members. And as this micro-culture continues to gain influence over a person's life, that person then becomes more and more isolated from those around them. Rather than moving into culture they are actually retreating from it, which is exactly what Jesus said not to do with His Great Commission found at the end of the Gospel of Matthew.

Suddenly you find yourself in this cult that is psychologically molding you to be like them, which then leads you to becoming more distant from mainstream culture. This, of course, is beginning to ostracize you anyway because you have such odd ideas and sayings. Pretty soon all your friends and your whole relational support group are found inside the cult. This means all your references for comparison are found in the group, therefore all the definitions of what is good and not good come from the group with no outside influence to interfere in their programming. They produce their own magazines, books, music, instructional media both audio and video, and they have their own festivals, conferences and seminars. It's like one-stop-shopping all within the group. When you encounter something like this, beware, because they desire to control you and all your input for information; if successful, they will begin to have profound influence on your output, that is, the decisions you make for living your life.

What is your output? What comes out of your mouth, how you behave, and where and how you spend your money. Ah, yes, nothing is free! Everything in these groups has a price they expect you to pay while also expecting you to continue giving to them with your tithes and offerings. It's really quite a racket.

We've covered a lot of ground in this chapter, starting with how these groups twist the meaning and concept of "church" so they can justify going about establishing their own church. This is irony at its most base form. They criticize church and then answer their criticism by forming their own group, hence, church! Looking back on this I find it quite absurd to criticize the establishment then go and absolutely imitate the establishment. So, word to the wise, if they criticize then imitate, they're probably not genuine.

Then we moved into simple tactics of vocabulary, thus language control. If a group wants to ban certain perfectly acceptable words or change their definitions, they're probably not genuine.

But wait! There are more tactics to be aware of.

CHAPTER TEN

Human Dynamics...
or...Simple Manipulation?

————+————

*"And can you, by no drift of circumstance, get from
him why he puts on this confusion?"*
— *The King, Hamlet, Act III, Scene I,*
William Shakespeare

*"Therefore each of you must put off falsehood and
speak truthfully to his neighbor."*
— *Ephesians, 4:25*

*H*ands drenched in dirty sink water I had to wipe them
off with a teacup-decorated dishtowel to answer the
ringing phone.

"Hello," I rasped.

"Hi, Craig, it's Tracey [not her real name]."

"Hi, Tracey, what's going on?"

"I need to speak to you and Nellie right after fellowship
tonight." Nellie [not her real name] was my wife at the time.

"Okay, what about?"

"I can't tell you now, you'll just have to wait. Good-bye."
Click.

Wait? What was this all about? Here we were a relatively young couple with a very young child and this "fellowship leader" was saying she wanted us to stay even later tonight than usual but wouldn't tell me why.

We met as a local group usually one week night and one weekend morning. Sometimes we'd add in additional meetings as well. This night was a Thursday night fellowship meeting at our leader's apartment. Now she was telling us, basically commanding us, to stay even later tonight even though we had a toddler boy and I had to be at work early the next morning.

The group used this tactic over and over again. It took me a long time to figure out why they used it and it took me equally as long to figure out why it disturbed me so much, but once I figured it out, the path for my departure began to become clearer and clearer. I guess you could call this tactic "make them sweat but don't tell them why."

Tracy was called our fellowship leader. She was basically our spiritual mentor in the Salem area and we were to be obedient to her, submitting to her leadership, because she had more training than the rest of us. The training, of course, was through the group itself and not through any accredited seminary or other institution of higher learning, nor was there any leadership or management courses typically offered to businesses and government that she had ever been to. Tracey, in many other contexts could have been a very good person, but she was not suited for what we would normally consider leadership quality. While she was trained by the organization, beyond this, she was barely high school educated, almost illiterate, and very slow to understand complex subjects such as philosophy, psychology, or science. But she was still our mentor and in the eyes of the organization, fully qualified to be a spiritual leader. We were to submit to her guidance regardless of how erroneous it may seem at the time. Typically, the corps of leadership she was a part of, actually called the Corps, were trained to see themselves and actually believed they were the spokesmen for God. The trouble is, what they spoke was organizational rhetoric and philosophy rather than true wisdom from God's Word. So they were really spokesmen for the overall leaders of the organization some three thousand miles away.

I am fully aware that education does not make a person more worthy of anything, our worth is in the price Jesus Christ paid on our behalf on the Cross, but there are certain gifts and traits people have that suit them to certain roles in life over other roles. Once a person begins to recognize their roles, or, as the Bible puts it, their gifts, they are certainly encouraged to pursue these gifts. This may mean more education, mission work, interning or volunteering, or a host of other options as well. There are several examples in the Bible of different giftings and places suitable for people to serve in the overall Body of Christ. This particular organization, however, considered everyone's gifting to be the same and if someone was uncomfortable or lacking in an area, that was the area to put the person into — their theory was to better round out the person by strengthening their weaknesses which meant putting people in places they are normally unsuited for and most likely not gifted for. So regardless of someone's comfort or confidence level, the organization put you in the place they wanted you and expected you perform up to expectations normally expected of people operating in their giftings. In other words, if they needed to plug a hole some where, they'd plug who ever was available into the hole regardless of their ability or gifting.

This concept is definitely not biblical since the Bible indicates each person has different gifts that are distributed by the will of God, not by the will of man. But think about it, if you get someone operating outside of their gifting, they're likely to lose confidence in themselves and then may become more compliant to the organization as the organization helps them improve by keeping them at the task they're not suited to or requiring they attend more ministry training to learn how to do the task. God's intent, however, is to gift and equip people to fill certain roles in His work so that we all have our unique qualities shining forth, giving Him glory. God wants us to operate in confidence and comfort. He wants this so much that the Holy Spirit is often referred to in the Bible as the Comforter! This organization didn't believe that and figured their job was to basically force people into doing tasks and assignments at which they were unskilled at or uncomfortable with. In other words, they disregarded God's gifting and put people where they could best serve the organization, not God.

Now back to this meeting.

Tracey was well suited for many other roles, but leadership wasn't one of them. However, being the ever-obedient servant of the organization, she accepted this assignment to relocate to Salem, Oregon, because there were no longer any organization-trained leaders in this area. Tracey, a single mom, dutifully loaded her little girl and beat up compact car and drove from Colorado to Oregon to become a leader. Just the thought of any organization sending a single mom on such an assignment is disturbing in itself, certainly not something any group that valued families would ever think of doing.

Tracey was completely opposite of Nellie or me. Both of us were college educated, I had been to graduate school, and my living revolved around grappling with and solving complex social, political, and at times, economic situations.

Tracey was also an individual who had a very hard and hurtful childhood, was robust of health, strongly opinionated and outspoken about those opinions, and she was very obedient toward —almost worshipful, really —of anything said by the leader of the organization. And, finally, Tracey had a tendency to have hugely unrealistic expectations of what people could accomplish, herself included, and she couldn't read people's temperaments for certain tasks or assignments with which they could be successful. She just gave orders and expected people to fulfill them, whether they had the physical make-up to do so or not, or whether they actually had the time to realistically do so or not. She was woefully equipped by her "leadership" training to know or observe anything in people to help them be successful, she was more trained on how to basically force people to follow orders. Perhaps Corps was a good name for them, although I know several other Corps (Marine) who take great offense over these folks calling themselves Corps.

But back to our story.

My personality tends more toward conciliation rather than confrontation, I am more naturally skeptical of leaders (I respect their positions, but until I see the actual fruit of their lives, I refrain from following them wholesale —this tendency certainly failed me in this situation, however), I am very analytical and desire to see the bigger pictures at play by knowing what preceded issues and then exploring all the ramifications of potential decisions before launching into them. I try hard to be sensitive to each individual and the nuances of their personalities rather than cram everyone into a box of "what should be." I sometimes take too much time to make a decision but at least when I make it I usually have a wide vision and understanding of the issues.

Nellie was more passive than me. Her health was beginning to deteriorate (she was diagnosed with fibromyalgia), and she expected me to step in and defend in any and all situations involving her.

Couple all this together and you have a very volatile mix for my wife and I with relationship to this "leader".

Simply stated, the evening was shaping up to a huge disaster, which, in hindsight, it was, in monumental proportions. I believe that was the night our marriage began to end.

After our fellowship meeting concluded we glumly followed our leader into her spare room (which was really her daughter's room she used for these types of meetings). In this meeting we sat for over ninety minutes while Tracey laid out a long litany of what she thought was wrong with my wife, and how she expected my wife to report to her in writing via email every week on her progress for improvement using ideas Tracey had come up with, and she expected me, the husband and head of my wife, to ensure all this happened under my roof. That last part was my key failure in my first marriage —abdicating my spiritual authority to someone else —but more on that later. At no point were we allowed to truthfully explain the health issues involved, the time constraints, and the fact that her solutions were suited to her, certainly not to Nellie. In other words, Tracey, bringing all her training to bear, said it's how she learned so that's how we'll learn. There was neither grace nor mercy in any word she said, and in the New Testament grace and mercy are prominent themes in every epistle. In fact, Romans says it's God's kindness that leads us to repent and not man's judgment (see Romans 2:3-4).

The sad thing about the meeting was there was no fight in us to defend ourselves, no fight in me to defend my wife. We had worried ourselves so sick plus we each had a big day coming up, we just wanted to get the heck out of there and quickly!

Why?

Simply put, tactics of manipulation.

But what do I mean by this? My theory is pretty basic. I believe people who are less than genuine in their motives and who are in authority over others or those who have some desire to take advantage of someone, will often say they want to meet with you but not tell you the reason. I believe they do this for two primary reasons:

One, so you will build up paranoia about the meeting and thus have yourself in such a tizzy of worry you'll automatically cave in once the meeting starts. You'll be so worried about possible exclusion from the group that your compliance factor with their desires will be in high gear; thus, the tendency is to agree to anything just to get the confrontation over with quickly.

Part of the success of this tactic is to make sure the conversation; confrontation as the organization I was a part of called it, starts off firm so if the person is cowering prior to the confrontation, they will cower even more once it starts if not completely cave in regardless of the absence of any fault or guilt. Stop and think about the nice people you know. Often they don't want to upset others nor be upset by them, they're basically people-pleasers; so once someone is upset at them, especially someone in authority over them, they fret themselves to near sickness over it. This fretting is compounded when the person of authority demands they meet with you at a later time, won't tell you the reason, and sounds firm in their demand to meet with you. Now you have time to stew over what this could possibly be about and all of a sudden your mind starts making things up. Before long you're condemning yourself for no reason and no verdict has even been rendered! All this is to breakdown the defenses so when the confrontation occurs, whether for legitimate reasons or not, the fretting person is mental Jell-o and will most likely not be able to hold his or her own once the tension gets released. They are at a mental cliff and ready to fall off.

Secondly, the ploy is to assure you have no opportunity to think up any kind of defense in the face of the pending confrontation. They have plenty of time to think up their accusations against you and their strategy with you for the confrontation, but they give you no such luxury. They want you to fly into it blind, completely unprepared, and they will not even give you time to come back later with a response, because they will want your response right then and there. It's much easier to win a confrontation when the opponent has no opportunity to prepare for it or time to respond to it. Plus, not giving you any opportunity to prepare pretty much assures them you'll have little to no rebuttal and you certainly won't be prepared for a solution, which leaves you more susceptible to their suggestions of how you should change according to their standards. Therefore, you're more compliant to their overall whims for your life.

I believe they employ these tactics so as to catch you off guard, thus making you more susceptible to not only their suggestions, but also to the continued authority they're wanting to exert over your life. And, of course, this authority is also over where you give your money and your time.

If their ploys are successful against you, it then is just part of the process of breaking down your spirit, your zest for life. In other words, it's a continual breaking down of your resistance to their demands upon your life. They can't use sleep deprivation or withholding necessities such as food or water, but they can and do psychologically manipulate you into compliance. It's psychological warfare 101; only the battlefield is living rooms rather than sports arenas or war zones.

This reminds me of a couple that was in my home fellowship group. They had been so beaten down by past leaders, Tracey being one of them, that by the time they were "under" my leadership, they started calling me on the phone for about almost every minor detail of their lives —it was like they were making sure they weren't doing anything now that would later result in yet another confrontation for them. They had had enough of that, but they were sticking around. Thankfully my style of leadership wasn't so harsh, but the habit pattern had been instilled and they wished no further painful scrutiny, but their programmed behavior put me in a spot of having to advise them according to the standards of the organization, which I didn't always agree with nor advise. Which of course got me into a lot of trouble, and, of course, into more confrontations, but it was still a long way before my last stand.

Now, is this how Jesus treated His disciples, in essence, His fellowship group? I think not, but for some reason, we allow ourselves to be treated in such fashion.

Jesus rarely rebuked His disciples. Rather, He encouraged them and empowered them, He let them be who God designed them to be, He didn't try to force them into some pre-fashioned mold established by some despotic leader thousands of miles away. In fact, what Jesus confronted the most harshly, as we've already mentioned before, is hypocrisy —those saying they were godly but were really anything but godly. Treating people with manipulative tactics with the intent of beating them down to submission to your whims is certainly not godly. And psychological warfare and tactics of mental manipulation are deceptive and thus born on the winds of lies, which of course emanate from the devil, the father of lies (see John 8:44). The antidote to lies is truth, and truth is from Jesus Christ who preached love and encouraged people to remove the beams or rafters from their own eyes before even attempting to remove the mite or dust speck from someone else's eye (Matthew 7:1-5).

Let's hearken back for a moment to the children of Israel. They were God's chosen people but chose on several occasions to rebel against God. Did God force them or manipulate them psychologically to do His will? No, He let them go the path they were choosing. He warned them of the consequences of purposely diverging from His path. After all, there is an arch enemy to God, namely the Devil who does indeed seek to steal, kill and destroy God's people (see John 10:10), but God let them be who they thought they should be even though He knew the Devil would try to slaughter them from the earth.

Now fast forward to today where people like you and me are honestly trying to seek God, to see His face, to hear His voice. Then come along these wolves in sheep's clothing trying to fool us, yes, manipulate us, into thinking they represent God with their whims, standards, and rules. If they were really of God, they wouldn't be so harsh or forceful with achieving their desires at our expense. So, considering they don't even follow after the example of the God of the Old Testament, further testifies they certainly are not of God at all. They certainly don't follow after the example of Jesus Christ from the New Testament. He exemplified love and in helping people where they were. He didn't lay guilt trips on people or invoke psychological ploys to get people to listen to or follow Him. He just loved and spoke the Word of God, and left the rest of the results up to God.

I've spent a lot of time going over these tactics because I think it's important for people to know them and to recognize them. It's not just cults who employ these tactics; many bosses do as well. In fact, a companion tactic is to start a confrontation with a complement, just to get your guard down. Then they let the real meat of the confrontation fly, just as you're relaxing and beginning to think everything is going to be all right. A common colloquialism for this is letting the other shoe drop. In fact, many corporate training sessions teach this approach as good, but the truth be told is when it's applied, the employee knows the complement was nothing more than hot air meant to get them off their guard. Thus, their boss is really just lying to them. Who'd want to trust that kind of leader? Think of the relational damage done to a person's soul when these tactics are regularly applied to your life. Not only will your confidence in yourself and in God be shaken, but so will your trust of people, especially those in leadership and authority. Which then of course, ultimately lessens your trust in the very One we should definitely place our trust in, that is, Jesus Christ. After all He did say to His disciples, "You trust God, trust also in Me." (See John 14:1.)

Again, we get back to Jesus Christ. He spoke truth to every one. So should we. So should our leaders.

CHAPTER ELEVEN

What is Worship and Who is Born Again?

———+———

"God is spirit, and his worshippers must worship him in spirit and in truth."
—*Jesus Christ, John 14:24*

"Offer your bodies as living sacrifices, holy and pleasing to God —this is your spiritual act of worship."
—*Romans 12:1*

It's a balmy August Sunday and the congregation gathers in a stuffy middle-school gymnasium for their church service. The music starts, the people stand, some have eyes closed as they sing, others lift their hands high in praise and acknowledgement, others just stand as the tears start to flow.

A famous Christian rock band from Tulsa stops in the middle of their high energy set to say some words of praise to Jesus Christ, then they sing of His deliverance and salvation. Many in the crowd respond similarly as the previous congregation —eyes closed, hands held high, some even tearful.

There's a man all alone in his den at home, on his knees with his face buried in a chair cushion crying out to God for wisdom on helping his son cope with life's tough challenges and the dad's strong sense of inadequacy of guiding his son through these challenges.

Are any of these worship? Do any of these responses indicate a saving faith at work in a person's soul?

A discerning heart or biblically wise soul would say yes to both. A cult, however, would say no, at least the one I was in would say no.

Why? They taught that true worship of God was speaking in tongues. "God is spirit and can only be worshiped via the spirit and that can only be done by speaking in tongues"[10.] They also taught that the only indication a person had of salvation was they spoke in tongues[11].

These are very critical issues because we all question if we're born again or not. If we aren't, then our eternity is looking very bleak and we would continue to struggle to find out how to be born again. And we, of course, want to give due acknowledgement and worship to our Savior and Lord, Jesus Christ, so we certainly don't want to go about our lives not worshipping Him properly. Then what are we to do?

The problem comes in with the fact that biblically, speaking in tongues is a gift not given to all truly born again believers, meaning each person receives different sets of gifts (or "giftings") from the Holy Spirit (see Romans 12:6 and I Corinthians 7:7, 12:4). Therefore, you may be indeed born again —or born from above as Jesus explained to Nicodemus in John 3 – but still not to speak in tongues. You will definitely have at least one gift if not several, but speaking in tongues may not be one of them. So it appears that each believer's gifting package may or may not include speaking in tongues, but nowhere in the Bible, in any version that I've ever read, does it ever say that speaking in tongues is the definitive proof of one's salvation anyway, so why should we all speak in tongues? It seems more of a dogmatic mandate of works rather than genuine service to the Master.

But what if you were in this cult and couldn't speak in tongues? You might begin to believe that you can't be born again for some reason. Thus you are evil and destined for eternal separation from Jesus Christ in hell. How comforting is that? This could be the final straw you have for Christianity and thus you just chuck the whole thing, cash in your chips, or just walk away for the last time. "Why bother," you say to yourself, "I'm not able to be born again anyway." Talk about handholding people onto the path of destruction. For you older heavy metal fans, this may be the on-ramp to the *Highway to Hell*. (And, I might add, there are other popular evangelical movements that also teach that all believers are empowered to speak in tongues, but they stop short of saying anything of it indicating genuine salvation. However, I still advise to be careful of such organizations. They may have ever-so-slightly stepped on the slippery slope toward cultism, especially if there is one dynamic leader over the whole thing.)

But what are gifts? We all know about the packages received at birthday parties and Christmas morning, but these gifts are from people to people. What sort of gifts does God give? It's a good question and one not easily answered, but let's see what we can come up with.

According to *Vine's Complete Expository Dictionary*, gift is the Greek word *charisma*. It means "a gift of grace, a gift involving grace." The root of *charisma* is the word *charis*. *Charis* means grace, or simply defined, it is God's unmerited favor bestowed upon us. We can't earn it and we certainly don't deserve it, yet, there it is, God's grace by way of Jesus Christ's atoning bloodshed on the Cross. Without His sacrifice, none of us could have salvation access to God so we obviously wouldn't be discussing gifts at all. *Vine's* goes on to say it is God's "free bestowments upon sinners" and "His endowments upon believers by the operation of the Holy Spirit in the churches."

Another set of authors defines spiritual gifts as "divine endowments; abilities God has given to us to make our unique contribution"[12].

My NIV Study Bible notes state that gifts are "referring to special gifts of grace —freely given by God to his people to meet the needs of the body." (See note for Romans 12:6.)

And the Life Application notes states "God's gifts differ in nature, power, and effectiveness according to His wisdom and graciousness." (Again, see notes for Romans 12:6.)

Eugene Petersen in the Message Bible states Romans 12:6 as such: "In this way we are like the various parts of a human body. Each part gets its meaning from the body as a whole, not the other way around."

But shop and compare for yourself with your own study of the Bible. The lists of spiritual gifts in the New Testament are found in: Romans 12:6-8; I Corinthians 12:8-10 and 28-30; Ephesians 4:11; and, I Peter 4:9-11.

Spiritual gifts, then, are endowments, or empowerments given to us from God. The lists in the Bible show several different categories from speaking in tongues, to healing, to helps, to teaching and pastoring, to hospitality, to evangelizing, and on they go. The best way I can figure to describe the gifts is to borrow language more attributable to genetics. When we're born again Jesus sends the Comforter, the Holy Spirit, into our hearts. As He, the Holy Spirit, inhabits our hearts, He is naturally able to communicate to our soul in ways that we'll understand and in ways that are totally unique to us. (Ephesians 2:10 states that we're all masterpieces in Christ Jesus, thus we are a one-of-a-kind original!) With this inhabiting of our hearts and infiltrating of our souls, comes the specific imprinting of the Spirit into our life —the special gifting package best suited to our uniqueness and function in the body of Christ.

The reason for this imprinting of special Spiritual genetics, if you will, is to enable us to function for God just as He purposes and just as is best for our mental and physical make-ups. God knew us in the womb so He would also know what was best for us regarding our gifts and special enablements.

Maybe some examples would help explain this a bit better.

Say for instance you're a naturally gifted speaker and have experience teaching classes or training adults or addressing large staff meetings. You've been going through life Christ-less and after years in the spiritual desert, you finally accept Christ as Savior and Lord. Pretty soon, as your walk with Christ matures, don't be surprised to be offered opportunities to speak in front of crowds for Jesus. Perhaps it's preaching at the Rescue Mission or teaching from the pulpit, or something else. God is using your unique gifting to advance His Kingdom through your specific talents. Or if opportunities aren't naturally coming your way, the Spirit Himself may nudge you to seek such opportunities, which could coincide with a gift of leadership or organization.

What if you like to cook but feel like that doesn't really lend itself to advancing God's Kingdom. Consider inviting Christian friends or non-Christians over to your house for your wonderful food. This would be in the realm of hospitality. Who knows, your kindness along with good food could very well be the formula to win a person, or entire family, to Jesus Christ —and all because you like to play with your food in the kitchen!

What if you're analytical and scientific? Often we feel that analytical and scientific types can't be Christians since so much of mainstream science rejects God altogether. First of all, there are a lot more believer scientists than we're aware of, and secondly, God created our minds to be analytical and scientific and He expects us to use them that way. He certainly can utilize these talents to His glory. Who better to explain that evolution is more of a religion than Christianity! Who better to show why it takes more faith to be a believing atheist than a believing Christian! Who better to show there is more historical and archeological evidence for Jesus Christ than Julius Caesar! An analytical person coupled with a heart of compassion could be the prime recipe for peacemakers.

Or perhaps God is calling you to a function or assignment that you consider way beyond any skills you have. Another set of authors state that God often gives a person an assignment first then the Holy Spirit empowers and equips him to fulfill that assignment[13].

So never underestimate what you or anyone else can bring to the Body of Christ. With each of us being a unique, one-of-a-kind masterpiece, there's no telling how much value your life and mine add to the Body of Christ.

But what are the gifts actually used for?

As you check the biblical references already cited, the gifts are to primarily help the overall Body of Christ. In fact, I Corinthians 12 compares the gifts to different body parts. While at any one time a specific body part may be more in need, it is only a matter of time before that part will take a back seat to a different body part. When you're driving, seeing is more important than tasting. When you're finding your way to the bathroom in the middle of the night, feel may be most important. Sitting at a fancy dinner, taste is certainly the star. Same with the spiritual gifts, at any given moment, given the need at the time, anyone's gift may be called up to the forefront.

But not all the gifts in operation are readily in view. Some work more in the background like helps and governments (organizational skills), while some are definitely more out front like teaching, preaching, and leadership. But all of the gifts are of equal importance, for if one is missing, the body is injured. You lose your tiniest toe, you not only limp, your balance is impeded. Suffer gallstones and your gall bladder or pancreas may become enlarged causing significant pain. If you can't eat for some reason, a whole host of problems arise. So it is with the gifts —each carries equal weight and has its importance in the divine Body of Christ, but no one gift is in the spotlight all the time.

With all of this stated, how harmful is it to expect every believer to be able to speak in tongues? If they don't have this gift, they may become so panicked about this one gift that they fail to utilize the actual gifting package they've been given. If this occurs they run the risk of really making no impact for God their whole lives when what God wants is to fill them daily with His presence and love. Or worse yet, they'll try to fake it, they'll just sort of babble to themselves and eventually convince themselves and others around them that it's real. Then how many other gifts will be counterfeited in this person's life? How much damage will this counter-feiting cause not just to the Body of Christ, but also to those who are being called into the Body but are not yet there? Remember earlier in the book we discussed hypocrisy? This would definitely be a refined form of hypocrisy, a new form we could call "gift-faking."

Gifts, as well as our whole manner of living, needs to be operated out of or motivated by, love. (See Matthew 22:34-40, Mark 12:28-31, Romans 12:9-10, and I Corinthians 13.) This love is both for Jesus Christ and for our fellow man. I find nothing at all loving about leading people astray regarding the spiritual gifts. It's not just anti-loving, it's anti-Christ. And if you track anything that is anti-Christ back to its source, it's always Satan. And if you track anything that at first doesn't appear to be anti-loving to Satan, it will always be anti-Christ and therefore anti-love —you reject Him who came in love, you reject love.

Plus, hyper-focusing on one gift gets people focused on that gift and only that gift; how it functions, how people admire you when you use it, and what sort of impact "I'm making" by using the gift. There isn't a focus on what the gift can bring for benefit in others lives and in the advancement of the Kingdom altogether. Nor is there any thought to how Christ will be glorified by the gift, it's just really self-glorification, I have the gift, so look at me!

Hyper gift focus will also cause a person to minimize the other gifts and most likely to minimize the people operating those gifts. So there becomes a potential of developing a little caste system of those who do and those who don't operate the gift. Or, as in this cult, people not operating the gift would eventually be asked to leave because they would be considered either too unbelieving to speak in tongues, or possessed by a demon that is blocking the gift from operating. Both of these are silly notions, but they are also serious notions and lies from Satan.

The first is ridiculous as established by this recent discussion — everyone gets a little different gifting package. The second notion is silly because Jesus gave us authority to cast demons out in His Name (see Matthew 10:1, Mark 6:7, John 14:12). So if there is a demon involved and the possessed person wants deliverance, guess what? That demon is gone in the name of Jesus Christ!

And, finally, hyper gift focus is really nothing more than a works-oriented mindset. This is clearly wrong because it's by God's grace we are saved and not of any works or efforts on our own and we live by faith and not works (see Ephesians 2:4-9, Romans 3:22-23, and Hebrews 11:6). If you research cults, however, you will see this as a common thread — that you are judged by your works. And, of course, the works are for the benefit of the organization, not an individual, or community, or for spreading the gospel of Jesus Christ. Being or becoming works-oriented is also a sign that a church is starting to lose its focus on Jesus. As a cautionary note to church shoppers, if a church has more stock in its programs and real estate than in its love and message for Christ, you may want to move onto your next door. If the church wants to do more for itself or it's image rather than to reach the lost souls and hurting hearts of the community, most likely they've asked Jesus to leave. Again, just keep on going past this church. And don't be fooled by a huge façade or packed parking lot. There are many churchgoers in our country who would rather have a social church than a Christ-centered church. And, if you're a member of such a church, find the courage in Christ to lovingly confront the appropriate leadership. You may help stop the slide, you may be asked to leave, you never know, but don't just give up on your church.

Now how about evidence, or proof of being born again? What evidence do we really have in our lives that prove spiritual re-birth? There's a ton, but much of it is very subjective and would be most fully understood by the person themselves and those closest to them.

For example, what about a transformed life? Someone who was a skid-row drug addict, atheist or fugitive. Now they're totally sober, Christ-worshipping, contributing members of society. Or the suicidal loner who's now a volunteer with the church crisis counseling ministry. Or the Apostle Paul, he pulled Christians out of their homes and had them carted off to their execution, who'd of ever known this notorious Christian-hater would receive such significant and life-changing revelations such as the Book of Romans and the Book of Ephesians.

What changed all these people? Was it a class or a seminar? No! It was Jesus Christ coming into their lives and the indwelling of the Holy Spirit, pouring out God's love into their hearts (see Romans 5:5). And, of course, it also takes effort on our part to no longer conform to our old ways of life and thinking, but to instead be transformed as we renew our minds to the truth in God's Word (see Romans 12:1-2).

But what if we accepted Christ even though our lives weren't in such dire situations? How do we tell then? If a nice guy gets born again, how much nicer can he get?

Evidence of the Holy Spirit working in someone's life can be all over the map. Someone may teach or preach an inspired message or deliver a powerful presentation of God's Word to a small group or a single individual. When a person is filled with the Spirit, the impact on the other person will be immediately felt deep in their soul. They may become tearfully thankful to receive the new birth or, as often happens, they may actually bristle, reject the message and even reject the messenger. Light, as it makes manifest darkness, causes the darkness to flee. As it flees, it may flee in a number of different ways. The person themselves may choose to reject the darkness, and thus, it flees out of their life, or the person rejects the message, which is really nothing more than rejecting Jesus Christ Himself.

In a large group the results of the Spirit would be a strong acceptance and affirmation of what is being taught. Perhaps this is shown via conviction occurring in someone's soul, someone who is yielding to the Spirit as He shows the person where he stumbled and what he must do to make it right. Such conviction could be shown as was with me as described in Chapter 23, an incredible outpouring of emotion and tears steeped in joy and relief! It could be people raising their hands or coming forward to accept Jesus as their Savior and Lord. It could just be a musical set moving the people to tears of thankfulness as the artists sing of Jesus' suffering sacrifices on our behalf.

Other results may include answers to prayers, but this is a risky indicator to rely on because God's answer to your prayer may be no. Even if you're the most honest, Christ-honoring person on the planet, the answer may still be no. God knows what's ultimately best for us in spite of what we might think.

But one indicator that shows up in every Christian's life in one form or another is fruit of the Spirit. Galatians 5:22-23 says the following about fruit:

"But the fruit of the spirit is love, joy, peace, patience, kindness, goodness, faithfulness, gentleness, and self-control. Against such things there is no law."

The Amplified Bible begins verse 22 "But the fruit of the (Holy) Spirit, [the work which His presence within accomplishes] —". What is indicated here is the fruit of the spirit is an inner working of the soul as inspired and empowered by the indwelling Holy Spirit. He moves in such ways so as to move the very hearts of men and women. The deep, unspoken urgings and desires of our soul to know Christ better are the workings of the Holy Spirit and the confirmation of His presence in our souls. The deep, driving desire toward forgiving that one person who hurt us so badly is the work of the indwelling Spirit; an unsaved heart is not moved toward forgiveness, but toward vengeance. That continuing thought compelling us to either stop doing something or start doing something is the Holy Spirit leaning in on our heart. All of these workings are ways the Holy Spirit clearly directs and influences human behavior.

Eugene Peterson renders these two verses in the following way:

"But what happens when we live God's way? He brings gifts into our lives, much the same way that fruit appears in an orchard —things like affection for others, exuberance about life, serenity. We develop a willingness to stick with things, a sense of compassion in the heart, and a conviction that a basic holiness permeates things and people. We find ourselves involved in loyal commitments, not needing to force

our way in life, able to marshal and direct our energies
wisely."
                                    —*Galatians 5:22-23 MSG.*

In other words, fruit within the believer really is indicative of deep and profound changes of the soul. Long and lasting changes in attitude and motive, in how you treat other people, how you approach worship, how you approach service, and even in how you approach yourself. Maybe for the first time in your life you will be able to see yourself as God sees you, as His beloved child. He came in the flesh, suffered, and died so He could know you; that heaven and earth were made for you and you were made for God; and that God knew you and had a purpose for your life before you were ever born.

And fruit is more than just change. It is growth. For instance, perhaps you've never really been a peaceful person but instead worry yourself sick (something cults prey on, by the way). God, by way of His Holy Spirit, can birth within your being a sense of peace and tranquility as you turn your worries over to God to guide you through. Philippians 4:4-7 is a great passage of Scripture to read about overcoming worry, as is Matthew 6:25-34. These passages encourage us to release our anxiety to God by way of prayer and specific request. As we do this, the Holy Spirit will then be able to replace that now lifted anxiety with peace, serenity, and a strong sense of trust that God will help us overcome and get through what ever obstacles there may be. We'll be able to sense God's presence in all our situations as we continually go to Him in prayer and specific request. We will feel an unconditional love and an abiding desire to know Him more.

Of course such changes don't occur over night, but instead take disciplined repetition and seeking after God. As your heart becomes more pure and your faith builds, these disciplines become second nature and your life is free as you have entered deeper into your relationship with Christ. Discipline of course, means work, but the Spirit, as you yield to Him, can direct your desires and motives to remain committed to the Lord and to see your commitment even increased!

All of these are indicators of being born again, all of these indicators are clearly lined out in the Bible so you need not be fooled by some cult or off-his-rocker theologian stating that you must exhibit one sign or behavior to prove new birth. If such charlatans appear in your life, you'll be able to say "chapter and verse". They won't be able to answer this challenge — but you will.

And you will be able to continue in the confidence of victory in Jesus Christ by knowing most assuredly that you belong to Him, that you are truly a child of God, and that you don't answer for your salvation to anyone but the Master Himself, Jesus Christ.

And as a final comment, do you ever wonder if those claiming to know THE sign of salvation are indeed saved themselves? I sure do. Thank God He's made the evidence clear so we don't have to wonder about our own eternal destination and we need not be influenced by anyone not speaking the words of Jesus.

CHAPTER TWELVE

I'm right... No, I'm Right.
How Do You Tell?

———+———

"A man should learn to detect and watch that gleam of light which flashes across his mind from within."
— *Emerson*

"All a man's ways seem right to him, but the Lord weighs the heart"
— *Proverbs 21:2*

The battle of right and wrong has waged for centuries, and dare I say, for eons. Every country thinks its right, every state, every county, every city, every person —we all think at one point or another in our lives that we have the answers. Sometimes we even feel if we don't have the answers, then they're either not worth finding out or we make stuff up!

Even comics reflect this reality.

Lucy Van Pelt, of the famous Charles M. Schultz comic strip Peanuts, is leaning against Shroeder's piano as he intricately plays a most complex Beethoven concerto. She says to him "I'm looking for the meaning of life. What do you think the answer is?" Without missing a beat, he thrusts a fist in the air with fury while shouting out "Beethoven! Beethoven is it, clear and simple!! Do you understand?"

Or how about Calvin and Hobbes on one of their philosophical Sunday diatribes. Climbing over logs and crawling through brambles, Calvin extols to Hobbes his good fortune for witnessing the pinnacle of evolution —himself.

What do these comics reveal to us about ourselves? They reveal that we are the centers of our own universe, that we sit on the thrones of our lives rendering judgment upon everyone and everything from that perspective. They reveal that everything in life is related to our way of thinking, that our perspective is, or at least should be, universal. Stated another way, my perspective, hence my reality, should be your reality as well.

These comics then, reveal, in a word, relativism. They also reveal selfishness, a view of the world with ourselves as the central point of comparison.

Relativism is the thinking that there is no absolute truth or no overarching moral code or moral structure to life. Instead, life is a series of personal constructs formed by each person's view of reality, or how they believe reality should be. In other words, what's good for you may not be good for me but it's still okay so long as no one gets hurt, and as long as you don't get in my way.

Another approach to this is if a person perceives something as being so, then that makes it so, it becomes their reality —and truth has nothing to do with their reality. Instead, they, like Pontus Pilate ask, "What is truth?" [John 18:38.]

Such an outlook on life can have far reaching ramifications negatively impacting many innocent parties. It reminds me of personnel problems in the office, personnel problems that darkened morale, spiraled health, and destroyed trust.

One of our human resources specialists used to always say, "Perception is reality." She said it so much that even our agency administrator, my boss, bought into it and continued repeating it again and again: "perception is reality." And what's scary, there's a lot truth in that phrase. Perception may indeed be a person's reality, thus, dictating their attitudes and behaviors, even to the detriment of others. It can be so strong that they even decry credible evidence contrary to their perception to remain clinging tenaciously to their distorted state of denial.

Chilling as it may be, consider the words of a well-know Second World War dictator: "if you say a lie loud enough and long enough, people will believe you." It's ironic and sad that the words of a dictator rang true in a social service office, but here's a definite case of it, a case clearly showing how someone's skewed perception of reality influenced the behavior of an entire office, and how perception can blind us to what we perceive as truth.

It all started with an employee of mine who was known for her bad attitude and sneaky ways. Somehow she was invited over to another employee's house for a party on a weekend. So here is an event occurring off work hours and off the work premises with me, the supervisor, having no knowledge of it. A few days after this party the house was robbed and the stuff that was stolen seemed to be selected carefully, like the culprit knew where to find it. Jewelry and musical equipment was gone and nothing else. The robbed employee blamed the bad attitude employee since she had a brother that she had admitted at one time burgled houses for drug money. But rather than confront this employee or have the police confront her, the one that was robbed waged an insidious underground attack that eventually affected the whole office. This attack included recruiting other employees into her hatred toward the suspect that eventually spilled over to me since I was the suspect's supervisor. But there was nothing tangible in the employee's performance that was any different than any other employee in a similar position. Even so, employees started talking bad about the suspect and would diligently search for ways to make her look bad, even to the point of possibly sabotaging her or fabricating situations to make her look bad. When ever they found something, or claimed they found something, they would run to the administrator and the HR person with their so-called evidence, stating how bad this employee was and lamenting how bad I was as her supervisor because I was doing nothing about this poor performing employee —and how could that be if I was really so passionate about the mission of our program? They yelled so loud and so long that they began to be believed.

And so, without any tangible evidence, my boss and the HR person now expected me to discipline an employee based on accusations plucked out of thin air and based on a non-work related incident that may have not even involved the suspect. Our boss didn't make the angry employee confront the suspect because he was lulled into thinking the evidence of employee performance was enough to render discipline, and the angry employee and her minions wouldn't stop. They kept on complaining and kept recruiting more high-level management —my peers —against me for not taking action.

Why?

Because their perception was their reality —this employee was bad and as long as I never did anything about it, with or without evidence, (even when I did take action they didn't know about it because personnel actions are kept very confidential) I was considered weak and a poor leader —I was the leader who built the program from nothing into the success it was, yet I was weak all because one employee harbored hatred toward another. It was a hellish time for my family and me —I was under so much pressure with no way to do anything to stop it that I began experiencing health problems. Plus I lost a tremendous amount of respect for people who showed me their worlds revolve only around themselves, regardless of the lack of evidence or the cost to others. And because of their perception of me, they had long-ago lost respect for me. So I had little trust for them or the projects they worked on and they had little trust in me as their leader.

So the self-fulfilling prophesy of perception is reality continued to fuel itself, day after day. Perception is reality, no mater how big a lie it happens to be based in or how flimsy the facts supporting the fabricated reality. And perception being reality leaves no room for grace and no room for redemption —it's this way and there's no way you or anyone can change that, so build the gallows and hang 'em high! Somehow, I don't think that's what Jesus would do.

But what about truth? Why isn't truth our reality?

Because truth doesn't fit into the framework of how we would do it. It doesn't fit into the way we want things to be, and truth won't allow for revenge. Thus we frame our own truth which in turn allows us to psychologically construct mechanisms for justifying and rationalizing how we behave within our own reality. In other words, we make up a world where we're always right and we never do any wrong, because if we were to face the truth we would see how fallible we really are. But instead, we have our own reality where everyone else is wrong, but we're always right. How many people have you met who live life this way? Several, I'm sure, perhaps even yourself. I know I've caught myself acting this way at times. It's like mentally maturing to five years old but no older —five year olds are notorious for seeing themselves as always being right and everyone else being wrong. They're also notorious for being the epicenters of their universe!

But what is it about truth that we find so difficult? Plenty.

Ask yourself, would you send the Savior of the world as a newborn babe? Probably not. Would you have a virgin pregnant? Probably not. Would you have the King of kings crucified on the Cross? Probably not. You, like me, would probably have the Savior of the world fly down through some sort of Steven Speilberg lightening and clouds special effect, and in doing this, no one would care about His mother. And rather than dying on the Cross, we'd probably have Him open up a can of whoop-'em on all those deserving it, you know, the bad guys getting wiped out in some spectacular show of fire and force with lots of explosions and smoke. But this is more Hollywood and make-believe than truth.

So we're left with **no**, we wouldn't do things God's way. That's why we struggle so much with accepting truth as our reality. We'd rather have things our way; hence, we'd rather see our perception be our reality —no matter what it costs others around us. We want whoop- 'em, not infants in mangers.

This is the ultimate of seeing through rose colored glasses —especially since truth is so much kinder and more freeing than our perception could ever be —yet live on in our cloistered perceptions we do.

We see examples of this all the time.

Consider various conversations you've had with people over the years regarding religion or spiritual beliefs. How often have we heard the phrase "I'm not into that, but if that's their thing, then great!" Or how about "if no one gets hurt, why should we care what they do or say?" Or, the quintessential cultural mantra, "if it feels good, do it!" How often has that one gotten many of us into a whole lot of trouble —we did what felt good and got grounded, or wrecked our car, or landed in jail, or worse.

And what about Creation versus evolution? There is insurmountable evidence proving not only Darwin wrong, but many of the so-called experiments proving evolution have been shown to be false or hoaxes. Yet as a culture we still go on believing the lies in the text books and the classrooms and school districts around our country tenaciously hang onto to what has overwhelmingly been proven to be wrong. Why?

Because since it's familiar, it feels good. In fact, even some major universities won't allow Christian schools to have their credits counted toward their admission standards.

Why? Because God isn't staying in the neat and tidy little box we've put Him in. He's defiantly not adhering to the standards we've set for Him. And also because their ingrained and subjective perceptions are their reality. Generations have been raised in these perceptions so they are now just accepted as truth and are not only being handed to the next generation, but are being blatantly forced onto the next generation — their perception is truth so it should be your truth as well. And, unfortunately, their perception, no matter how wrong it is and how often it's been dis-proven, has a hugely negative impact on a large segment of well-educated high school students who have great potential for bringing more good into our country. Yet the universities are telling them 'no' because what they've been taught doesn't fit their perception of reality. So not only is their perception reality, it is also now their standard for systematized prejudice and discrimination. They're really not institutions of higher learning, but institutions of systemized indoctrination toward atheism, almost gigantic cults for leftist-liberalism and spiritual oppression. Their specialty should be called "applied reality." They take their reality and apply it to everyone else around them. If you don't subscribe to their reality, they just deny you entrance. They don't engage in discussion or try to learn from you, they just tell you to go away.

Or consider politics. Many organizations want to pass laws allowing for their behavior or special interests to flourish, and if these are unbiblical, then the Christians say so and campaign against the laws. But what happens? The Christians, or other religions, but mostly Christians, are called bigots and accused of forcing their beliefs on others, when in fact they may be actually trying to stop laws from being forced onto the masses that the masses oppose anyway. But the bottom line for this discussion is the main premise to promote such laws is "it's our right to do what we want." This attitude, of course, totally denies any overarching moral code and the individuals promoting such laws see themselves as the definers of moral code. They expect the rest of us to agree and to willingly follow along with their moral code.

It's not unlike the many despots the world has already seen. So many of them promise utopia —as long as you do what they say! Many political action groups are the same way. They want to whittle away our right to free speech while legalizing all the things they want to do while making it illegal, or at least very uncomfortable, for us to speak against it. What they're doing is giving themselves liberties with culture while telling us we have no right to speak about it unless we support it, even though we're still in the same culture they're trying to influence.

Perception is reality.

What does all this have to do with cults?

A lot! The same tactics used by cults are used in these other examples. But what cults do is try to get you to think that the church perception of Christ is wrong. Hence, Christ isn't God in the flesh, but a man, a great man, but still just a man. This means that another man can now come along and if he is successful in getting you to question Christ's deity in your mind, then he can subtly take Christ's place upon the throne of your thinking with his sly and convincing doctrine. Just like the angry employee or the special interest political groups, if they yell loud and long enough, and if you listen to them, you may begin to believe them. And if you begin to believe them, then maybe you'll begin to follow them. And if you begin to follow them, then maybe you'll begin to contribute money to them. And after that, maybe, just maybe, you'll begin to serve them —thus perpetuating their doctrine and their lies, without them ever having to do the leg work in your neighborhood or workplace.

Another question is why are there so many thriving cults today? Because someone yelled loud and long and eventually picked up more yellers, and eventually larger numbers of people listened to them. But the tricky counterfeit is that what they're yelling, like all such movements, have traces of facts in them that get you hooked into what they're saying. You think to yourself that they sound kind of like the pastors I'm used to so maybe they're just more tuned in to truth. But if you spend much time looking at their facts, you begin seeing they're just a bit distorted. And if the facts are distorted, then truth is flat out missing in action.

What does that mean? It means the angry employee was operating out of an assumption that in turn developed into her perception, thus, her reality that eventually dominated her thinking and behavior. While it wasn't truth, it was a mental attitude directing her actions, but no one dug to the deeper truth that perhaps was based in jealousy or the sense of competition. The angry employee had a shred of fact that the suspect had a bad attitude —the truth was that the bad attitude employee was facing significant family crises, which shaded her behavior. The fact for the political groups is we do have individual rights, but the truth is they're taking away one set of the population's rights to get their special interests legalized to become rights and to then shut those up who speak against their special interests. The ironic thing is their special interests aren't illegal, they're just not recognized with the status, or label, that they want their interests to have.

Cults operate with shreds of facts as well. The primary fact is that church in the United States is filled with lukewarm Christianity, stated another way, many people calling themselves "Christian" but not living that way.

So, rather than going after the fringes of society like political action groups, cults go after those on the fringes of the churches. After all, many churches are less than Christ-like anyway, so there's a large market for disillusioned would-be churchgoers. This is the prime demographic for cults. I'm sure most people unfamiliar with cults think they target mainly lower educated and less intelligent people, but let's face it, that demographic doesn't have the money of the disillusioned middle-class. Plus, statistically speaking, the middle-class is the most generous socioeconomic class in the USA. And, on top of that, once we find something we support, we keep on giving to it —we're a faithful lot once we make up our minds to give.

But back to the churches.

How many of us have walked into a church only to feel isolated, out of place, or on display because we're not a usual face in the church lobby? The climate is more a cold front than a warming love emanating from a depth of Christ in people's souls. The looks on people's faces are more of inconvenience with having to shake your hand then the looks of genuine welcome and thankfulness that you've come.

How many times have we heard so-called Christians using the rhetoric of hatred while arguing with an atheist? I've seen and heard unbelievers behave with more love than many people calling themselves Christians. Or how many times have we seen so-called Christians talking of another segment of the population with great disgust and venom? Instead of figuring out how to reach this segment, they condemn them stating how they're judged already. Nowhere are they attempting to understand why people are the way they are, they just expect people to be like them, and when they're not, then they're to be ridiculed. Certainly not a trait Jesus exhibited.

And what about worship services that are no more than ego-fests for the musicians or directors? It's more of a performance than a band of musicians leading a worship service of praise and thanksgiving to God.

Or, and this is my biggest concern for the western church: how many pulpits ring with no more substance than what are politically correct or hollow feel-good affirmations? Or we see more of them on TV wearing Rolex watches while begging for money. Or the name-it-and-claim-it preachers who have large congregations merely because they boost everyone's self-esteem but bring no true spiritual challenges or maturity to the people?

I would say Jesus is in none of these churches — that's why the masses are increasingly disillusioned with Christianity. The churches themselves are turning people away, they're looking for Jesus and finding instead, elitist social clubs or shallow euphemisms for deeply hurting people. When you need release from sin, what good does it do if a preacher in an expensive silk suit tells you that you can do all things in Christ? While this is true, just saying that with no specific ministering to the sin will result in a hollow-feel-good emotion, but once the sin re-enters the person's life, they'll have no strength because they've received no coaching for how to resist the sin itself. Affirmations are nice, but affirmations on their own are as empty as cracked pots — you pour your cold water into them and the water just runs right out on your shoes. What have you accomplished? Nothing but frustration and soiling nice shoes. Jesus instead soiled His shoes by walking in their steps, He took time to minister to people's hearts and souls, He didn't extol pious platitudes of hot air, He extolled genuine love and compassion for the human condition.

At some level all of humanity longs for substance, but so often we come away with only fluff — just surface-level, watered down quips and quotes, the same drivel and dross we see on TV night after night. It might be dressed up in flash and fancy, but there's no meat, no depth, no life-changing profound testaments regarding the ugly state of the human condition. And there are certainly no suggestions or solutions for changing that ugly state into anything remotely attractive, much less really beautiful. There's especially no discussion for how some of your mess is your own doing!

All of us are broken at some level or another and we're striving to find fixes to that brokenness —addictions, reckless behaviors, and religious hypocrisy are all symptoms of a broken humanity, of a humanness that is lacking in depth and meaning. But in today's culture, the offered solutions of addictions, sexuality, or religious hypocrisy usually result in nothing more than hurt compiling upon hurt. We risk our souls, get hurt, then drown our pains in some sort of salve TV or grocery store magazines purport, but again these drive us deeper into hurt and deeper into our self-centered excuses. And as long as we focus on ourselves or on what culture has to offer, there will be no healing. There may be superficial theatrics or momentary feel-good days or hours, but long-term we're not only back in the same pit of hurt, we are actually deeper into that pit, and the deeper we get, the darker life becomes.

But along come the cults. They make you feel welcomed, they offer a general sense of acceptance with no judgment (at least at the beginning), and they also have a "doctrine" that seems more meaty than what the church is serving up. They even have a way of making you realize that you are somewhat responsible for your own predicament. That alone lends them more apparent genuineness or credibility than you found in the church on the corner. So off you go, to explore what they have.

But before we get to that, how do we know who is right and who is wrong?

Ultimately, we have to rely on God Himself as He works through the Holy Spirit to direct our thoughts and paths (see Proverbs 3:5-7). But here is a list of things to check for, things that should be based on truth rather than just perception, or what someone wants your perception to be, things that should sound loud alarms and raise gigantic red flags in your thinking.

First and foremost, do they embrace the deity of Jesus Christ? If not, they're definitely not representing the genuine

Savior and Lord of mankind. They are, as mentioned in earlier chapters, trying to bump Him off the throne of your life only to put themselves there in His rightful place. No deity of Jesus, no authentic message of Christ.

But wait, there's more! Just in case they either don't reveal what they really believe about Jesus, or shroud their thinking in profound-sounding mystical psychobabble, the list goes on.

Do they extol empty euphemisms and airy affirmations? Do they claim lofty states of happiness and success but have no firm biblical foundation for their assertions? Are their sermons laced with a bunch of examples and less-than-believable illustrations with little or no Scripture references or reading? Then they're probably wrong.

Do they act harshly or judgmental when questioned about their beliefs or when someone in their group screws up? Are they highly critical of other churches or well liked evangelists or other highly regarded Christian figures? Are they equally critical of typical orthodox questions about Christianity? If so, they're probably wrong.

Do they consider themselves to have the ONLY right doctrine on Christ and the Bible? Do they claim to have a founder who had "special" revelation from God? Then they're probably wrong.

Do they leave no room for grace or redemption? Are they always quick to claim evil rather than broken human mistakes? Do they act like restoration has to be earned rather than bestowed through God's mercy and grace? Are they quick to condemn the "less fortunate" of our society? Then they're probably wrong.

Do they speak highly of themselves at the expense of other people or organizations? Are the only props the ones they get by putting others down? Then they're probably wrong.

Do they behave in a way that is contrary to your view of Jesus? While this is a risky analysis and should always be paired with other observations, there are times when we know that something done or said is NOT what Jesus would do. If we view an action or word that is contrary to anything we've seen in Scripture it could simply be nothing more than a mistake, a misstep or misstatement. But if it happens more than once or is part of a larger highly orchestrated event —like a festival or a larger gathering of the organization's members —it is probably a true view of their beliefs or mission. Thus, they're probably wrong.

While this list isn't exhaustive nor the only one in existence, it is here to help keep you out of pitfalls that folks like me have fallen into. This list, however, is not intended to be a lightening rod for criticizing genuine Bible-believing and Christ-honoring churches. Please always remember that people do make mistakes, and one thing Jesus would do is to allow for mercy and grace. But these items on the list, especially when one or more are present and persistent, are a very good indicator to you and others that the organization is not promoting the Jesus of the Bible, that they're not bringing a message of hope, love, and deliverance, but a message of oppression, control, and bondage. To be sure I state it clearly I will state it again. If items on this list are present and persistent with an organization, you'd be highly advised to steer as clear of that organization as possible.

But sometimes we do get sucked in. If that happens, how do we know?

CHAPTER THIRTEEN

Setting the Hook, and Other Inner Workings

—✝—

"For my yoke is easy and my burden is light."
—Jesus, Matthew 11:30.

So, there I was sitting in the living room of a married couple I didn't know waiting for "the class" to start. In the room were two card tables set up with tablecloths and three chairs at each table. The chairs were arranged so we'd all get a good view of the alter —the color TV set sitting up on a stand in the corner of the room. At each place were a syllabus and a couple of books "given" to us as "gifts" from the organization. Funny I thought even back then. I had paid for this class out of my own pocketbook and yet they were saying they were giving me a free gift. It would have been more honest for them to have told the truth, that the books were included in the class fee. But no, they were trying hard to get me to think of them as benevolent and as extolling favors to me —favors to better my life, when what they were really doing was setting a hook into my soul that would then be used to lead me where they wanted me to go. So I guess I missed another big clue right in front of my face, calling something I paid for free. It's just like on TV when you see one of those commercials that says you get some widget for free, plus shipping and handling. Plus shipping and handling? Isn't that just another way of saying the widget ain't free? But back in that late March of 1985 these thoughts didn't occur to me. Evidently even though I was recently graduated from college I wasn't cynical enough yet. Instead, I merely wanted answers about God, answers to questions I had since that fateful night of the blowout when the "voice" saved my life, when a seat belt became a symbolic emblem for a lifelong journey toward God. Little did I know the "answers" I would get in this class would send me on a detour of distraction, a wrong road lasting nearly sixteen years, leaving in its wake destruction, despair, and desperation.

But in 1985 I thought I was getting answers to questions that I hadn't had answered in the churches or from the religious people I knew. In fact, I didn't want religion, I wanted truth, but as described in the last chapter, I wasn't appropriately "armed" with the right questions to ask about truth. And all the questions I had about Christianity certainly revolved around God, the Bible and Jesus. But as you've probably guessed, no one was able to answer my questions in ways I could understand. No one seemed to know how to answer the question of how was Jesus God? I was always told to read the Gospel of John or take it on faith, or they'd just get defensive and huff off while others called me a heretic then huffed off (huffing off was usually involved!).

But what are the answers? How can I read the Gospel of John and just "get it?" Apparently people weren't familiar with the Scripture in Romans 10:14 where believers are encouraged to explain this stuff to people, not just slough them off to someone or something else. Perhaps it's ignorance of Scripture or perhaps it's just laziness, but few Christians seem to be able to actually explain Scripture to a seeker. And I don't tout myself as some great scholar, but at least I gave the gentleman at the Rescue Mission something to think about, something to grasp. And what about the Apostle Philip and the Ethiopian in Acts 8? The Ethiopian is reading from Isaiah, and then Philip comes along side him and asks, "Do you understand what you are reading?"

The Ethiopian answers, "how can I unless someone explains it to me?"

So what did Phillip do? Did he huff off? Did he call him names? No, he sat down and explained it him. We are to do the same. We are to explain the Scripture to people and when we have trouble, just admit that and tell the person you'll get the answer for them —then be sure to follow up on this or you'll just develop a reputation of speaking but not doing, something that still plagues the church today.

Well, this organization was aware of the above Scripture references and certainly set out to exploit them for their own purposes because they sure convinced me they could answer my questions and more. Thus, they were definitely preying on me, a disillusioned with church middle-class working stiff —the very profile they desire to hook.

So off I went with these folks who said the class would answer my questions. I couldn't believe it, but here I was sitting in a class that was supposed to usher in not just understanding about God, but the actual power of God in my life. Who would of thought that Joe-Party dude like me would be in a Bible class, but I was excited and ready for the answers to flow. I had been seeking God for years and thought I was about to find Him.

Perhaps another item to add to the list at the close of the last chapter is: if it sounds too good to be true, it probably is.

This particular organization greatly touted its class. It was the class that gave you the answers you needed. It was the class that led you into experiencing the power of the Holy Spirit. It was the class that would help you "unlearn" all the error you had already learned. And the person teaching the class was affectionately known as "doctor" or, "the teacher". As I would later learn, it was highly questionable this person ever earned a Ph. D. He claimed he earned it from some small seminary in the Colorado Rockies, a small seminary that had for some mysterious reason burned down. But even among the records that were saved, there was no record of the "doctor". And actually promulgating the use of the phrase "the teacher" in regard to the Bible was, in retrospect, the height of personal conceit, for the One called the Teacher in the Bible was none other than Jesus Christ Himself. Again, it was all about knocking Jesus off the thrones of peoples' lives so he could plant himself there, to replace truth with his doctrine, his twisting of the truth.

I've already covered quite a few aspects of this class, so I'd like to give a little insight on the way the organization put the classes together, this process was also a huge clue that these guys weren't the real deal for Christ.

Rather than handing out tracts or other pamphlets explaining how their approach to Christ set you free, they insisted you take their class. You'd first be invited to attend one of their home fellowships. You'd feel welcomed there, but it wouldn't be a surprise to find one of the more "mature" believers hovering around you trying hard to figure out what traditional or orthodox aspects of Christianity you believed that they then could try to refute. Once they zeroed in on these aspects, they would then start attacking these traditional believes, beginning to show you why they were lies. They would do this to get you to believe that they had the corner on the truth, which, of course, would be explained more in-depth in the class that you could register for right now. You had to have the class to begin grasping the depths of truth from God's Word while simultaneously grasping the treachery of the lies you've believed all your life. Thus, the very church in America was steeped in lies and all the teachers in the pulpits of America were knowingly dishing out lies and were therefore serving Satan, not God.

Wow! Quite a load to hear in your first involvement with the group. But they had a way to get the disillusioned to indeed question the authority of the organized church; they were, after all, disillusioned, and therefore easy prey. They had a way of planting enough doubt in what you'd already heard and learned that you in turn gave them a hearing. You gave them a shot at explaining God, the Bible and Jesus Christ. And since this was usually done in a small group in a home rather than a sermon being shouted from afar, it was more intimate and easier to grasp. You could make eye contact with the person, you could ask questions, and, yes, there was the opportunity to feel acceptance from the group as they rallied around your dawning comprehension of how lucky you were to be in their presence and pulled out from the fiery lies typically preached in your average American church on the corner.

The hook is slowly being set into your soul and you are not even aware of it either. In fact, regrettably, most of them aren't even aware of it. They all think, just as I did, that they are doing the Lord's work, that they are the light breaking through this darkened world of a mystical Jesus' and a wrongly divided Bible. But how could this be when it took so much work and suffering to even get a class started? So what isn't revealed is the ugly underbelly of the organization and their requirements, their demands, for holding classes in the communities. All you see is the nice, clean home with happy followers of the organization. You never see the intense struggle it is to get a class up and running.

It starts with the headquarters in Ohio sending out their trained leaders through the country. To show their audacity, their leaders are called Corps, not c-o-r-e, like the center of a matter, but C-o-r-p-s, like the Marines. But some of their disciplinary tactics were not unlike the Marines. Anyway, these corps would be rated on how many fellowships they could produce in a community and the fellowships were produced from the classes run in the communities. But, to run a class, you were required to have at least seven people fully registered (this means they've paid their class fee —nonrefundable I might add). Seven, according to "the teacher", meant spiritual perfection, so obviously the class had to have a minimum of seven participants.

Here's another hint about cults. If they are reliant on numerology, that is, seeking spiritual significance through numbers, then they're probably wrong, or at least sorely misguided. Jesus never relied on numbers; He relied on the leading of the Spirit and the truth contained in the Word of God.

Well, to get a class together, the corps person would put pressure on us non-corps people to "get people registered for the class." This meant for us to maintain a favorable status with the corps, we had to hustle basically anyone we knew to register for this class, whether or not they had any interest at all in Jesus or Christianity. We had to continually badger people who showed even the slightest interest. I remember that as we were nearing the five-o-clock PM deadline to have a class ready, I had to call a person several times in one day. The first phone conversation he told me he'd get back to me, but since the corps person was being rated on meeting an artificial deadline, I had to call this person hourly through the day until he was so exasperated with me he never talked to me again. But, this was somehow my fault rather than the distant HQ or the corps leader and her acute paranoia.

We also had to go door-to-door to muster up interest in the class, and going door-to-door is another sign of a cult, not to mention one of the most uncomfortable experiences you can have. Imagine invading people's privacy with a message they don't want to hear —I have many horror stories about going door-to-door. At one time, a corps leader told me to pick a fight with someone at their door on the Trinity and watch them back peddle. Now how is that loving? But it was easy to do because most people can't discuss their faith intelligently, so along come some spiritual predators and they are easily overwhelmed. Did that get people in the class? Of course not, but it did generate animosity and give true Christianity a black eye, because, you see, we said we were Christians so that's how we were judged, as representatives of Christianity, thus, as representatives of Jesus Himself. No wonder Christian groups get doors slammed in their faces all the time; we tick people off!

Another time we were "witnessing" door-to-door in a large apartment complex in the suburbs of Portland, Oregon's largest city. I was the group leader and in my group was a son of a corps leader —the heat was on to deliver. How would I perform under this pressure and how many folks could I get registered? As it turned out, none —duh! But I did have the police called on me and the apartment complex manager in her Trans Am chased me down, which was easy to do since I was on foot. Boy —was that exciting! I heard this vrooming, then screeching, as she power slid her car to a stop! Swinging her door open she leapt out yelling for me, the leader of the group. As I approached her she literally screamed at me to leave the premises immediately, because we were trespassing and the police were on their way. That certainly got my attention, because as a government employee the last thing I need is trouble with the law.

Now, isn't it convenient that the corps leaders weren't the ones being chased down or having the cops called on them? They were probably in some residential neighborhood where these things don't happen. But there I was, thinking I was doing the Lord's work in suburbia and now being threatened with arrest after being chased down by a shrieking woman in a muscle car. What could I do? How was I to respond to this latest threat? I considered my options very carefully and, thankfully, made the right decision —we left, thankfully before the cops arrived. And, admittedly, this made me look pretty good in the eyes of the corps folks; I made such an impact the cops were called! Not sure that'll go on any resume, though!

But that shows how important it was to get a class going, that the corps leaders, while not in the middle of the fray themselves, were still willing to send their "apprentices" (that was me since I was considered a "non-corps" leader) and their own children out into harm's way to please the HQ that was over three thousand miles away, an HQ that had no clue how folks in Oregon lived their lives, nor, frankly, care how they lived their lives.

It was not uncommon, however, to have only one or two people registered for a class for over a year before we were "allowed" to run a class on an exception basis. (Read 'exception' to mean 'failure'.) But when we did run a class, oh how we basked in the victory and the fact that we were running a class and others weren't. Again, how is that loving? Or, we would combine a class with two or three different areas combining their registrants. This usually required that some "new students" had to drive considerable distances to take the class. But if they were at all late, they would be expelled with no return of their registration money. Plus, they set the schedule and expected you "to believe God" to either get the time off work or to secure the adequate child care, for kids were not welcome at the classes unless they were in the class (or were the corps leader's children). In other words, the class did not operate with compassion or an understanding of real-life circumstances. They just expected you to adjust your life to them. This was hugely indicative of what they would expect from you and your family from there out — you just didn't see it coming yet.

But back to the class. The rhetoric of the class was laced with high-sounding words and with learning about the power of the Holy Spirit. The teacher talks on the video tapes a lot about receiving power from on high, and, as previously explained, this guy taught that the only way to exhibit that power was to speak in tongues. Whether that was true or not, and it's not, it was a huge presumption on his part that he had the corner on the Holy Spirit and on understanding the giftings of the Spirit. But then again, this is the same guy who claimed that God told him that God "would teach me the Word as it had not been known since the first century if I would teach it to others"[14]. Whoa! Say what!? Isn't this claiming greatness above the likes of Martin Luther, or Thomas Aquinas or St. Augustine?

This is a reminder of one of the big clues in the list at the end of the last chapter. If the founder makes huge claims to exclusivity, they're probably wrong, and dare I say, greatly influenced, if not possessed, by demonic spirits.

But none of this crossed my mind in March of 1985, I was just waiting for answers. And, boy, did I get them. Not only was this person hyper-focused on speaking in tongues, but he also systematically tore down all the main tenants of orthodox Christianity. I've already spent a lot of time on their views of Jesus Christ not being God, but here are just a two more tidbits to be aware of and protected from if you encounter them somewhere down the line.

Mary is the mother of the divinely conceived Jesus, therefore she's a virgin, but this guy convolutes and distorts Greek language to state that she wasn't a virgin when He was born. This is clearly against Scripture (see Isaiah 7:14, Matthew 1:18, 24-25; and Luke 1:26-35), but he was so convincing that he was believable. He also claimed that hell was nothing more than a lake of fire that the condemned would be thrown into. Once in the lake of fire, they would have a momentary experience of tormenting hell then be annihilated, snuffed from all existence, thus they would have no more consciousness. They would just cease to be, which in turn means he taught there was no eternal torment or eternal separation from the presence of God. This is contrary to what Jesus spoke. He taught that hell is a place of eternal torment, not a momentary existence just prior to complete annihilation. He clearly stated hell has raging fires and the worm that doesn't die, as well as saying the "unsaved will be thrown outside into the darkness where there will be weeping and gnashing of teeth" (see Matthew 8:12; 10:28; 13:40-42, Mark 9:43-44, Luke 16:19-31, and Revelation 20:10-15; another great resource is Randy Alcorn's book called *Heaven*).

There are certainly several other examples, like claiming they can teach you how to overcome doubt, worry and fear. They fail to tell you that it is the Spirit as He works in your heart that brings this fruit into your life (see Galatians 5:22-23). Our peace comes from Jesus. He is the one who gives us peace that the world cannot give (see John 14:27 and 16:33). But if you don't believe that Jesus is God in the flesh, the very author of peace, than how can you really trust Jesus, a mere man, to give you peace? Basically, you can't. You wind up manufacturing it in your mind, convincing yourself you're peaceful when what is really going on is the rapid onset of an ulcer at the back of your throat or in the tissue of your upper intestine. Denial is never an answer Jesus purported to anyone at anytime. And just the very nature of corps leadership disturbed your peace because of how intrusive they were.

I could go on but hopefully I've made my point.

But now that the class is over, what was life like in this cult that didn't have a commune or compound with barbed wire fencing and guards? Just how did they exert control over your life? What could possibly be used to keep people thousands of miles away in check?

CHAPTER FOURTEEN

Distant Control and Local Hurting

———+———

"Those who look to him are radiant; their faces are never covered with shame."

—*Psalms 34:5*

*G*uilt. Plain and simple, guilt is the great crusher of the will, the snuffer of individuality, the grayness that pours over our Technicolor lives. It casts its dulling hues over every surface until all that remains is a colorless world of duty and demands. Along with guilt comes its equally life-sucking companion, shame. Shame is the destroyer of dreams, the breaker of the spirit housed in each soul, and the author of self-hatred. Shame is the black hood of execution pulled over our souls, lulling us into its clawing clutches of condemnation, darkening our lives into nothing more than mere meaningless existence.

This destructive duo is the air cults breathe. The byproduct of this air is the shriveled and decayed environment of fear. Fear paralyzes and stifles and is the ultimate promulgation of the devil himself —paralyze the masses then mow them down like so many budding dandelions on a green spring lawn. This destructive duo reduces the vibrant human soul down to nothing more than a chess board pawn —used and used up for the purposes and schemes of the distant board master, the one making the moves that you wind up having no choice of questioning or abandoning. They tell you what to do and you do it —or face consequences. Your sacrifice is nothing more than another means to their desires and your pain and suffering is not even a wisp of air that raises the hair on their arms —you are nothing but a tool. No soul, no will, nothing, just a tool, a tool with a wallet and two good hands.

Sounds harsh. Sounds like slavery. Sounds like the horrors gripping parts of the third world or obscure fringes of distant cultures that traffic humans. It sounds like something that would be so obvious the authorities would come and shut it down immediately and cart away in chains the minions responsible for such deplorable treatment of humanity.

But cults are obviously not so, well, obvious. Their ploys are primarily psychological and are geared to play to your desires to please God while also exploiting your disillusionment with the established church. They weave an intricate tapestry of plausible doctrine with slowly increasing injections of expectations, of works, of duties and demands. They also shroud their lies in cleverly quoted "research" or references to the original ancient manuscripts —manuscripts none of them have ever seen and whose existence is questionable. They also use biblical references or illustrations as persuasion techniques using such phrases like "the Word says that..." and then fill in the blank on what ever it is they want from you. Or maybe, now that the class is over and you're somewhat hooked into the organization that so graciously taught you what you now know of the Bible, they'll say something like "don't you remember in the class how 'doctor' said..." then proceed to convince you that since it was in the class it is expected of "mature believers" like you. Or if it wasn't in the class specifically, they will try to twist their desires relative to examples from the class, likening their desire to some specific segment in the class or to something in the class they know moved you. In other words, the hook is set and they're luring you in, manipulating your desire to please and be accepted into the more mature portion of the group.

But what sorts of things would they ask of you?

In this particular organization there are well-documented allegations of forced subjection for certain folks domiciled at the headquarters or any of the other campuses owned by the organization. Such forced subjection even have accusations of sexual contact and other manipulation deemed necessary by whichever leader was seeking the subjection. I don't know if any of those accusations are true, but for us in the "field," that is, in our own homes living our own lives away from any property or campuses they owned, their methods of control were usually rendered through their corps leaders and didn't have such overt subjection. No, our subjection was more along the lines of works, monetary giving, and obedience. In Chapter Ten I attempted to discuss how the organization used manipulation in the context of meetings — confrontations, really — and getting us to either worry ourselves sick or to attempt to keep us unprepared to fight back. But there were other tactics as well. Here I will attempt to show how they exerted universal control over the entire organization, control that actually led to a lot of hurting and very bad decision making by those under the control of the organization.

From the pulpit of the headquarters auditorium, the main leader at the time, (we'll call him Carl), began to teach on two subjects he wished to blend together for the next few weeks: tithing and living debt-free. They sound pretty harmless, and these themes certainly fit within the framework of a culture that is spiraling more and more hopelessly into the deep and dark abyss of debt, bankruptcy, and destitution with each passing second and each cash register scan of plastic purchases.

We are a culture obsessed with spending way beyond our means. If we want it now —and we always do —but we don't have the cash to cover it, no worries. Just whip out the old credit card, slide it through the gadget that asks for you PIN number, sign a little piece of paper, and off you go, with another purchase that will most likely wind up in a heap in the garage or tossed in the garbage because it broke apart. "Meism" and "consumerism" have partnered together to wrap a chokehold on the average American budget. Not only do we struggle to pay our bills just to live, but we can't keep up with our plastic purchases either. Nor can we keep up with our stuff and junk. We have so much of it we fill up garbage dumps at record numbers and have to rent mini-storage units because our garages are too full of all that stuff and junk.

So, yes, our culture is collapsing under its own weight of stuff and junk. And with such stuff and junk we have lost the meaning of what really matters in life. We have replaced God, family, and other relationships with stuff and junk, with greed and workaholism to pay for that stuff and junk that our greed convinces us we need, and we have totally shelved our God, our families, and our very souls.

So, yes, our culture is at a terrible crossroads of needing to wake up out of our consumer stupor to again breathe in afresh the cleansing nature of God, the revitalizing essence of family, and the fulfillment of strong friendships. We need a clear call to return to our roots, and our roots are in God.

So, yes, the teaching subjects sound like great beginnings of a cultural revolution for returning to our primary values while shedding the shackles of stuff and junk. But is this really Carl's motive? Is he really that concerned for the broader culture of the nation? Or for the collective conscience of Christianity? With a little deeper information one really begins to question his motives, one begins to see that he isn't concerned at all for the masses and his teachings will prove to be anything but harmless or helpful.

Just a few years prior to this teaching, the founder of the organization died and after his death all sorts of turmoil erupted throughout the organization. Power struggles ensued, finger pointing was rampant, and in the wake of this, several leaders and their own regional followers left the organization. With their departure went significant amounts of revenue, thousands of people leaving the organization equated to hundreds of thousands of dollars of funding stream drying up. Essentially, the organization was facing a situation of economic disaster. Now those of us on the field never really knew where our "tithe" money went, but later accusations indicated good chunks of the money went for superfluous luxury for the founder and his most loyal followers, like Carl. There was even a time when the founder of the organization had a fancy motor coach, a couple of Harley Davidson motorcycles, and there was a private jet as well. Of course all his bills and other incidentals came out of the tithe money but no one ever got to see the "books." They would often refer to reputable CPA firms looking through their books, but we never heard this from the CPA firms themselves or got a glimpse of the books for ourselves. A budget was never published or even referred to and there was never any forecasting shared with us. In other words, we mailed our tithe checks three thousand miles away and never saw the results of such giving. We just knew we had to give because that was God's law —or so they taught us anyway.

But when the revenue streams began drying up, so did these luxuries. They were slowly sold off to help pay the bills. They still never opened their books but did start complaining about money becoming scarce. Sort of the old adage, when you want something, guilt people into it.

Not quite recognizing this history at the time and still trusting the leaders of the organization, those of us in the field sat with rapt attention to either phone hook-up dial ins, where we gathered at a central location to "dial in" long-distance to headquarters to hear the weekly teaching; or listening to the weekly audio tapes of the teaching mailed out to us from headquarters. It was pretty much expected we'd do one or the other. In other words, it was not acceptable to miss a Sunday night teaching service either live or through the week by way of the mailed tape! They were so concerned about people listening to the teachings, that fellowship leaders, especially the corps leaders, would frequently quiz their fellowship attendees to try to see if people were listening to the tapes or not —if it was discovered they were not, guess what? Yep, you guessed it, there'd be another one of those back room chats.

And as another aside, if you sponsored one of the dial-ins in your own home using your own landline, you paid the bill. The organization, even though requiring it, wouldn't foot the bill for it. We were expected to tithe to them but when their requirements generated more personal bills and expenses, we were expected to pay that ourselves too. Luckily we sometimes set out a cup for people to put money in that the host could then use to help pay the bill —and sometimes the dial-in lasted two or more hours, so the bills could be quite high.

This particular night, after some rather stiff music and a bunch of announcements nobody cared about, Carl began to teach. His style was more of a yelling football coach-type style than anything. Now and then he did have some funny jokes, but he was mostly either trying to tell us what to do or was teaching a variation of one of the twisted biblical doctrines established by the founder to which the organization clung tenaciously. He also used this pulpit to state very strong political opinions, even to the point of stating if the U.S. were truly serious about dealing with the Middle East, they'd just drop a bomb on them and start over. Somehow I don't see Jesus suggesting that. He might even be pounding the table with his sandal at this suggestion!

On this evening he started off by teaching that a minimum every believer should give monetarily was ten percent. That was what the Old Testament standard said before the Mosaic Law was rendered. Therefore, since it pre-dated the Law, it applied to us. I'm still not sure I understand that logic other than just plain manipulation, but back then a whole bunch of us bought it. How convenient! Here's an organization that always taught the Old Testament was for nothing more than our learning, now all of the sudden saying that, well, some of it is to be applied to our day and time and that part just happened to about tithing. Hmm, makes you wonder.

Now don't get me wrong. The New Testament does not say we don't tithe. In fact, in II Corinthians 9 the Apostle Paul is clearly teaching about giving generously. I'm also not saying it is wrong that church leaders, pastors, ministers, and the like, should not be paid out of the giving —quite the contrary. In fact, ministering to God's people IS their job and they are to be paid by the tithes and offerings of the congregation. The requirements for them, however, would be are they teaching truth and are they honest with the money —meaning every cent is accounted for and not just put into a discretionary account with one name on it and no further oversight!

But the Old Testament only being for our learning, according to this organization anyway, also applied to the Ten Commandments. Isn't that interesting, how is it the Ten Commandments were only for our learning and yet tithing was to be strictly adhered to? Of course, these types of questions were not encouraged to be asked, and if they were asked, they were answered with psychobabble or, more aptly put, doctrine-babble. They'd hem and haw and burble out something like the Ten Commandments were only for Israel but King Melchizedek established the standard of ten percent in Genesis 14, which predated the Mosaic Law. So that meant this particular commandment was for all believers, not just Israel and that's why the ten percent standard applies to us today.

Huh!? A whole bunch of commandments predated the Mosaic law but I guess I just didn't know that back then.

But that was only half the teaching, the other half was about being debt-free.

It seems most theologians agree that debt is not a sin but it is to be avoided if possible and the way we handle our debt will determine if it becomes a sin or not. If we have debt then we are to honestly go about paying it off, while being mindful that, because of the provisions of debt, we are beholden to our agreements of debt. Thus we are expected to abide by the agreements for payment and if we break those agreements then we are subject to its consequences (foreclosure, repossession, collection agencies, etc.). (See Matthew 18:24, Proverbs 6:1-3; 22:7.) And Romans 13 seems to further encourage us to pay our debts while understanding we'll never be able to pay back the biggest debt owed, that is the debt of love extolled by Jesus Himself on the Cross. He died to pay for our sins and that's a debt we can never repay, even though a true Christ-follower will do his or her best to exemplify the love of Jesus to others. Just because we can never repay His debt of love to us doesn't mean we become unloving. Quite the contrary, because of His love, we are expected to be loving.

This organization, however, taught that debt, no matter what kind, was a sin and for us to be able to function as God wants us to, we had to pay off all of our debts. We never learned about the debt of love but we certainly heard ear-fulls about the debt of finances. The organization was so serious about this that one key requirement for taking their Advanced Class, the class they wanted all their "disciples" to take, was you had to be debt-free, and if you weren't actively desiring to take the Advance Class and working diligently to eliminate your debt, there was something wrong with you which would most likely result in you being bounced out of the organization — marked and avoided as being disobedient to the organization leadership, in a word, rebellious.

They expected you to own your cars outright, which meant most people in this organization had cars that could barely run, and they even frowned upon educational loans, the ones that aside from a mortgage, take the longest to pay off for most middle-class Americans. And, let's face it, other than the wealthy, who can afford to pay college tuition out of a monthly paycheck? And to deny families access to college education, well, isn't that really just promoting ignorance? Many a dictator has said that keeping the masses ignorant is a major tool to keeping them oppressed. Why did Stalin go to such lengths to destroy all literature but Soviet doctrine? Why did Hitler have such a systematic way of indoctrinating youth with Third Reich rhetoric? Look at Pol Pat or Castro, or Hussein. All of them had some sort of mechanism for keeping the masses ignorant, which in turn made them easier to oppress while also managing to hide the opulence in which they lived —oppress the masses but take their earnings for your ease and comfort.

Hmm, I wonder... Even the founder of this organization encouraged his "students" to set aside all secular reading material but the Bible and his teachings about the Bible for three weeks. Why? Because several studies on human psychology suggest it takes about 21 days, three weeks, to break old habits by replacing them with new habits. Other cults encourage the same sorts of things (funny this is, so do diets). Just read what the founders want you to read and you'll achieve some sort of enlightenment, but their meaning of enlightenment really means nothing more than obedience to their commands. If you read nothing but their materials, then you're less likely to know what else is available or grasp that their way isn't the only way, or that their way is just flat wrong.

It's easy to see that at first blush the teaching appears almost noble, an organization trying to protect its people from the constriction of debt, but they're just going about in a bit of a misguided way. Like they just went a little too far but at least are teaching people to be careful with their money, to make wise purchasing decisions and to be wary of long-term financial agreements.

A deeper look reveals a different landscape, a landscape never really mentioned, even by the organization's detractors, and maybe even a landscape only I've come up with, which means it may be wrong, but the timing is just too suspect for me to let go of as a unique coincidence. Perhaps people have been too blinded by their own debt that they can't see the nefarious motives behind these teachings, but again, discernment is a gift of the spirit so perhaps this is a strong dose of that discernment —that thousands of people were lied to in order to extort money from them to save the organization from complete bankruptcy. Such extortion also saved the organization's leaders from needing to go out and get real jobs themselves so that they could earn their own money and give. So they stumbled upon a way to use guilt and shame as tactics to bring more revenue to keep the organization afloat.

But people with debt don't usually have a lot of money to spare, so what do you do? You take your teaching to a level of requiring people to sell off what they can to eliminate that debt, and, of course, to augment the cash-flow.

What's the biggest debt most of us have? Usually our homes. But what do homes have along with owed money? Equity. When you sell a home what does equity translate into? Surplus. What does this surplus mean for this organization? What Carl just got done teaching about —tithes. And tithes mean bolstering a revenue stream that is drying up. Perhaps I'm too cynical, but when you see the revenue stream dry to a trickle then Carl, the supreme leader of the organization (his actual title was Reverend and President), teaches to become debt-free, including selling homes that are not owned outright, it looks suspicious. Walks like a duck, quacks like a duck…you know what I mean.

And how was this enforced? You guessed it. The corps, the local henchmen of Carl and headquarters —not unlike the mob and their hired thugs who beat on you until you pay what is owed to the Boss. And boy, did they apply the pressure.

I remember being in one fellowship where this nice couple owned a manufactured house. Granted, it wasn't a typical home constructed on a vacant lot in a residentially zoned area, but it was theirs and had their name on it. Plus, manufactured homes were really quite nice and were moved to many residential lots, as this one was —slap down a foundation and place the manufactured home on top of it, and instant neighbors! Most of the rest of us were renters and only wished we owned a home and thought their home was quite cozy and nice. But what happened to this couple was darn near close to a crime. The corps leader, Tracey again, sat them down and strenuously told them they needed to either pay the thing off or sell it —she employed both guilt and shame. Since this was the teaching of the leader it was then an edict from God, and who did they think they were keeping this home after such a clear edict?

Of course they couldn't pay it off, otherwise it would be paid off. So they faced a huge dilemma: either submit in obedience and sell the home or risk being ostracized if not excommunicated from the organization for disobedience.

This organization had a practice that was called "mark and avoid." This meant that if a person left the organization or they got kicked out, then all remaining members of the organization would "mark" that person, meaning observe what happened to them and why; and avoid them, actually shun them. This is very similar to excommunication but was different in the fact this action was usually taken over disobedience to ministry doctrine rather than biblical doctrine —as was mentioned earlier, they were primarily deemed guilty of rebellion and needed removing to keep others from being equally tainted.

As explained in earlier chapters, most of us desire to belong to some sort of a "people group", whether it is a healthy family, church, cult or gang, or even a ball team. We have a strong sense of belonging and anything threatening our standing in the group is a very real threat and danger to be avoided. So this strong desire for belonging can definitely be manipulated to the favor of the organization. Thus they come up with some doctrine that "must" be adhered to and if it isn't, then the "mark and avoid" process becomes a very real possibility and an excellent tool of coercion. Therefore, those belonging to the group probably have a strong desire to remain belonging to the group so they will reluctantly comply with the group's demands, even if it means going against those pains we get in our stomachs when we know something isn't quite right, like adhering to some stupid fraternity or sorority initiation ceremony, we put up with it so we can belong to the group when its over.

But such compliance only comes with continual reminders from the corps leader to do what is required. With enough continued bombardment and veiled threats of mark and avoid, the pains in the stomach are ignored (until the ulcer hits) and compliance is acquiesced with head hung low. It is like a defeat being dealt by your own weapon.

So after weeks of being "taught" the right doctrine and the consequences for not following it, this couple put their home up for sale. Their home was the only investment this family had and they were being convinced, if not threatened, to sell it and thus rid themselves of all their investments into their own future for the sole reason of wanting to continue belonging to the group. Oh sure, the organization was trying hard to convince us this was God's will, but God doesn't mark and avoid, only the organization does. Only rarely did God call people to actually give up their homes, especially when they were hard earned and well kept.

So, up went the "for sale" sign. Weeks went by and the house didn't sell and didn't sell. The corps person was getting frustrated with it even though it wasn't her home or her dream. Her dream was to be ordained someday and she didn't want this couple to cause a demerit on her record, which most likely would happen if one of her "charges" didn't do all they could to become debt free, and, of course, tithe the badly needed equity. She wanted her record to show how "in control" she was of her people and how obedient she was to headquarters. She even went as far as accusing the couple of not trying hard enough to sell it or believing big enough to sell it. So no matter what the couple did or didn't do, it was wrong and the corps person was going to be sure they knew it. Nowhere was there mercy or compassion for a couple giving up a home they had only a few years ago dreamed about and had scrimped and saved to actually buy. And here they were going through the trauma of selling a home because some organization three thousand miles away told them to.

At last the home sold and the couple had a bit of equity and nothing else to show for it. But rather than celebrate the sale or take a big breath of relief, the corps person instead felt it necessary to remind the couple to tithe off the equity. No time to ponder or pray over it, no time to even mourn they had just sold their home and couldn't go buy another one. It was just write the check! So now they had to empty ten percent off their meager profit. And because they weren't wealthy and able to buy another home outright, the organization, by teaching all debt was sin, clearly established they couldn't reinvest in another home. That meant they were facing capital gains tax penalties! What a deal, sell a home and fork out up to forty percent to the organization and the government. Just what god was this organization serving anyway?

Funny, none of us asked that question at the time. None of us stopped to question just how far out of reality this organization and their teaching was about a mortgage being a sin of debt. None of us dared to pose the issue that a mortgage was really an investment. Sure it was a monthly bill with interest, but as most of us know, as the property appreciates, so does its investment value, and considering this home was in a nice Eugene neighborhood it was sure to appreciate.

But no, obedience was the path of least resistance and the path of expectation for remaining in the good graces of the organization. So, understandably, they chose that path, losing their home rather than choosing a different path and being labeled "mark and avoid" and cast out into the cold, cruel world.

A similar, though not as drastic, situation happened to my family and me.

When my first wife and I were married, she brought to the marriage many things including a car that ended up being quite a clunker and a money drain. This in itself is quite a story but seeing as how this is a longer chapter I'll get to the point.

The final time this car broke down it was towed once again to the garage with mechanics we trusted. I was so frustrated. I had previously drained our small savings account to pay repair bills and had at the last breakdown cashed in the cash value of an insurance policy to pay that repair bill —remember, debt was bad so I couldn't do like everyone else in the world —put it on my Visa card and pay it slowly. Being at the end of my rope both in patience and finances, I asked my mechanic what needed to be done to get the car running reliably? Couldn't we just do one big-time overhaul and be done with it? Just what was it going to take to get this thing road-worthy?

"Sell it," was his answer.

That certainly surprised me! That's why I liked this mechanic, he was gruffly honest. Oh, he knew this car was a money-pit but instead of encouraging me to continue pouring money into it and into his garage, he simply said get rid of it. He said it was the "car from hell" and could not ever be reliably repaired. Why? It had evidently been totaled previously to my wife and her first husband buying it. They of course didn't know that, but looking at the lines of the car being varied (one door jamb had a wide separation from the frame while on the other side the door jamb was very thin), plus different colors of paint beginning to poke through indicated it had been in quite a wreck. And, finally, he said the piston shafts were slightly angled which meant the frame of the car had actually been bent. All this meant the car had been thumped pretty good and was basically un-repairable, if not worthless.

So now what do I do? Who wants to buy a car that doesn't run?

Well, even though I was in a cult, I truly thought I was serving God and He did still make His presence known to me —we traded the car in, sight unseen, for a used SUV. I was honest with the car dealership too, but somehow they decided to give me trade-in cash for the car. Now, of course, we needed more cashola than just the trade-in value, so what were my options?

I could go get a car loan. Oh, right, sin was debt so that was a 'no'.

I could ask Mom and Dad for money but that was just another loan and, besides, I didn't want to ask for any more money than I already had because of this car.

I knew I couldn't knock off a liquor store or mug an old lady with a big purse. I had no stock to sell and I didn't want to become a drug pusher, so what were my options?

I only had one: cash in my eight-year-old individual retirement account. Oh man, it seemed so logical then, but just think what that IRA would be worth today (although I would have lost half of it in the divorce). Even so, if I had a loan back then it would be long-paid for now but I would still have the IRA earning money for my retirement. What a huge mistake to have cashed in an investment that wasn't geared to pay off until I was in my late fifties but was instead cashed out in my thirties. Plus since I cashed it out long before maturity, I had hefty tax penalties, so I only wound up with just over half the value of the investment —which meant I probably really only broke even with that money. So this possible retirement account really turned into nothing more than a complex and penalized savings account.

Bad, bad decisions all based in the desire to obey God and remain in good standing in the organization. Such control they exerted in the name of God when I don't think God ever condoned any of these actions. And, yet, through these poor judgment and bad financial decisions, I'm still alive and still able to serve the true God.

But look at the cost to these two families.

Anyway, I think you get the point. Through this whole car-clunker process good ol' Tracey kept reminding us we just needed to believe God for a vehicle —somehow though, I don't think God would necessarily condone dumping an IRA instead of what the rest of the world does —get a car loan! But that's what we did, and that's why I stated that Carl's teachings were anything but harmless. Here are two examples of people obediently cashing in investments that would have paid huge dividends in the future if only they were held on to. Instead, one couple is now renters and not earning enough money to buy another home now, and I cashed out a retirement account for an SUV that has long-since stopped running and is probably scrapped in a junk yard somewhere.

But through distant teachings and local control, the organization, knowing people want to belong to some sort of people group, exerted almost despot-like control over their people to do nothing but serve their own desires. They definitely employed the dynamic duo of guilt and shame, leaving in their wake shattered dreams and empty bank accounts.

CHAPTER FIFTEEN

Freedom or Abdication?

———+———

"Jesus Christ was an extremist for love, truth, and goodness."

-Martin Luther King, Jr., Letter From Birmingham Jail.

"It is for freedom that Christ has set us free. Stand firm, then, and do not let yourselves be burdened again by a yoke of slavery."

-Galatians 5:1.

"So if the Son sets you free, you will be free indeed."
-Jesus Christ, John 8:36.

Or how about another famous quote: "We hold these truths to be self-evident: that all men are created equal; that they are endowed by their Creator with certain unalienable rights; that among these are life, liberty, and the pursuit of happiness." These words are, of course, from the Declaration of Independence signed by the Continental Congress in Philadelphia on July 4, 1776.

Why such lofty quotes in a book about cults? Perhaps because what cults do best is enslave; by insidious manipulation they usurp our freedom, they drain our free-will, they dehumanize our individuality and suffocate our independence. They somehow cajole us into joining them through airy promises of knowing the truth, getting closer to God, or even experiencing a freedom we have not yet known. But after they hook us they instead begin a systematic way of trapping us into a clandestine web of connection and expectation that is inordinately difficult to escape from. They intertwine themselves into the very mesh and fabric of our lives that to rip away from them is akin to ripping a piece of our own soul out; when in fact, what they have already done is just that —unknown to us they have ripped out some of our soul, replacing in the remaining vacuum their own life-absorbing edicts and tactics.

Anthropologists and psychologists the world over have written essays and observations on the human desire to belong to something. Much of this book has been spent writing about the very same thing. Most of us desire to belong to something or to someone. One of the biggest reasons is meaning —we struggle to find meaning in life. The second biggest reason is we strive for significance in our existence. We crave meaning and we desire significance.

If we can become part of something meaningful then we have significance because we are advancing a meaningful cause, or participating or even leading a significant role in that meaningful cause. We now have substance to our lives and substance to our souls. We now feel like more than just another one of the six billion inhabitants on this planet. We're now "somebody", we're now important; and we shout within our souls "Look at me, I am significant, hear me roar!"

But have you noticed? The world doesn't just dole out significance on a daily basis. In fact, in our culture, we pound out the messages that if you're not gorgeous, not rich, not famous, then you're not significant. If you're not a great athlete, or a famous actor, or wealthy businessperson, you're just not that important. If you don't have a big house, drive a cool car, or have all the latest fashionable clothes and gadgets, you're just an average Joe, a run-of-the-mill person of no particular impact. And, let's face it, by these standards; most of us are not any of these things so we face the daily deluge of dealing with our insignificance.

Advertisers make gazillions of dollars convincing us to buy their products so we can gain some shred of this fictitious material significance. Television is packed full of talk shows of people telling us how great they are so we can feel even crummier. Then these same shows go about telling us how we can be like them so we can then perhaps bathe a little bit in their significance, which will then hopefully lend a little significance to us as well. And there are of course books upon books on how to be something other than yourself because "your self" is not significant.

So then much of our lives are driven in part by very strong desires to seek meaning and to find significance. Advertisers know this. Hollywood knows this. Politicians know this as well and use it to get us to campaign for them even though we'll never meet them nor probably ever benefit from any decision they will ever make.

Even college recruiters know this. They'll tell a talented young prospect how much prestige they'll receive just by going to their school.

We even know this at some level, that's why we want to be seen at certain events or with certain people. They're important so if I'm close to them then others will think I'm important as well!

But guess who else knows this? Of course, cults. As the previous chapter explored, cults enslave our minds and our wills through guilt and shame. We saw in the last chapter how their control can be so extensive that they can influence the financial decisions we make, even to the point of making bad decisions or dissolving lifetime investments.

But their control goes much beyond that. Their control can even get into the very intimate nature of our private lives. While I'm not exactly talking about sexual intimacy —although that too can be impacted indirectly because of stress —I'm talking more about how we treat each other behind closed doors in the privacy of our lives because of the influence of the teachings and directions of the organization's leaders. We listen to their teaching tapes, go to their twice-a-week local fellowship meetings, read their books, and even subscribe to their magazines. We're absolutely surrounded by their doctrine. Thus, their influence, which, with enough exposure, will saturate every detail of our lives, including our marriages and how we raise our children.

I had briefly touched upon this in Chapter Ten. Remember back then, when my wife and I were called to the back room after fellowship to listen to our leader outline what she thought was wrong with my wife? How we had been so beaten down by tactics that we had no fight left in us? How I didn't even come to the aid of my wife who was being figuratively choked by this so-called leader? Remember how I had alluded to spiritual abdication and that I'd get to that later? Well, it's later! It's time to discuss the greatest sin I committed in my first marriage and how that sin lead to an accelerated slide into marital oblivion.

My greatest sin in my first marriage was abdicating my spiritual authority. What, no adultery? No physical abuse? No second mortgages to cover secret gambling debts? No hiding behind newspapers or TV sports every night? Nope, none of that dramatic, front-page headline stuff for me.

Nope, just plain old abdication, basically caving in, handing over my God-given authority as a husband and father to an organization looking out for its own best interests and not my family's.

But just what is abdicating? According to my trusty Thesaurus, it means, "to relinquish, surrender or give up one's power." Wow, how apt, definitely describes what I'm trying to get at! But does this mean that I just crumpled in a fit of extreme "wimpy-ism"? Or that I just threw my hands in the air and yelled out, "okay, fine, do it your way!"

No, in fact, according to personality type indicators, that is highly unlikely to happen as I'm considered more of a champion who is highly motivated if not somewhat non-conformist or fiercely independent[15]. Something just doesn't seem right though. How can a fairly strong personality abdicate any kind of authority? Isn't abdication akin to weakness or some sort of moral failure? Isn't abdicating more for the milk toasts or wallflowers of life rather than for those who like to grab life and live it to the fullest? Perhaps, but not quite.

So how does it happen?

Simply put, slowly, very slowly over a long period of time.

Plus, as stated before, my personality tends more toward conciliation rather than confrontation so I look for solutions and common ground, tending more toward idealism than, sadly, realism. I try to see the good in all people and since I'm an idealist, I can be easily tricked into thinking something is good when it is not, unless I pay close attention to that small but discerning voice in the back of my head that often yells out "danger, danger!"

God will definitely warn His people who are heading into danger. The problem is, the cult has slowly ingrained in your thinking that if there is any thought contrary to their instructions then it is a thought that is really contrary to God's will for your life. I know it sounds silly to imply the cult actually does your thinking for you, but in a way it does because coupled with its classes are the leaders promoting over and over again the doctrine as laid out by the top leaders at headquarters, and, of course, their doctrine is motivated in its most common denominator by self-serving and self-propagating desires. And, since many of the local leaders come from headquarters-sponsored training programs, all they know is what the organization taught them. What they're basically taught is obedience and tactics of control to assure obedience.

For instance, my fellowship leader, Tracey, told me a story about her time "in residence", that is, living on the campus of one of the organization-owned properties they used for their schools. People who were in residence were expected to work while also paying tuition for the classes. And the only way they could have their tuition paid was to be sponsored by people who sent in money monthly earmarked for her tuition — if she wound up being short, she would eventually be asked to leave. She wasn't allowed to work secular jobs to earn money toward her tuition, and she certainly wasn't allowed to get loans; no, she had to "believe big enough to get people on the field to sponsor her." The program was considered training on how to be a leader back out in the field. What they learned was, as stated before, the doctrine of the organization with a few research classes thrown in for legitimacy to be considered an accredited two-year college, which was weird because none of the credits were transferable anywhere else, at least not that I was aware of.

Once a person graduated from this program, they were labeled a "corps graduate" and were ready to be assigned wherever the organization deemed necessary for them to go. Usually corps grads were sent to areas that seemed ripe for "winning people", which was really a euphemism for recruiting people into their classes. As explained earlier, this was one of their main vehicles for hooking people into the organization and into giving money to it.

Tracey was a single mom while in training. Her location was in Indiana where the winters can get very cold. One winter night, her leader awakened her at two in the morning to go drain sap from the maple trees. Never mind she just had lights-out at midnight because of a large study load and workload, never mind the temperature with wind chill was hovering at zero Fahrenheit, and never mind she had to be out of bed at six. She was rousted out of bed anyway with less than two hours of sleep to go perform a task that was impossible, drain sap from frozen trees. But ever-dutiful she did it. She didn't get any sap but she obeyed. She never made it back to bed because she got back to her room just before six and only had time to get her little daughter up (who was evidently left alone while she was draining sap), take her daughter to day care, go to her other job then go to classes. This is all evidence of classic cult control by sleep-deprivation as well as separation from her young daughter. They had strictly controlled environments, including eating and childcare. No wonder these folks came out so calloused and cold —they willingly endured horrendous treatment, allowing themselves to be bossed around into doing impossible tasks for seemingly no reason other than they were told to do it.

They even taught meal etiquette to such a degree as to humiliate you for holding your fork wrong or eating a chicken leg with your fingers! To me, if you have to eat a chicken leg with silverware, well, it's just not worth eating at all. Next thing you know they'll want you to eat a hot dog with knife and fork.

Needless, to say, such continual tactics of deprivation and control brainwashes them, if you will, into thinking these tactics are okay. So this all leads to them applying the same doctrine and tactics on you, at least to a degree; while they can't tell you to go perform an impossible task at 2 in the morning, they can tell you what to do and think regarding activities and behaviors and then go about whatever means they feel necessary in order to control you into conformity, thus assuring your obedience.

If for some reason you begin to think totally for yourself and operate in the freedom that is actually in Christ and guaranteed in the founding doctrines of this nation, they threaten you with the ever-so-near mark and avoid tactic. Therefore, complicity is your only option for continued belonging in the group. You think all you have to do is comply and all will be well, you'll be a member in good standing plus they'll leave you alone, giving you some peace from their seemingly endless prattle of suggestions. In fact, without even noticing it, you find yourself subconsciously accepting their "suggestions" as commands; phrases such as "why don't you try" really mean "you need to do such and such." After so many such suggestions with the subsequent back room chats for not taking the suggestions, you just begin taking the suggestions as orders, just like the staff sergeant immediately implementing the friendly suggestion just rendered by the general. And let's face it, life is easier that way and you can once again answer your phone or go to meetings without fear of ambush.

You never stop to think that such compliance will only bring a false and temporary peace with the organization while bringing a real war in the rest of your life. And it is only temporary because as you comply with one suggestion, another one will soon follow, and another one after that, and so on. For such people fancy themselves experts or at least knowledgeable of any field or situation life throws at you. Usually the suggestions are a controlling mechanism since each suggestion has attendant with it a means for "reporting back" the progress for following the advice. When you don't follow the suggestions, because you thought that's what they were, just suggestions, you tell them so since you're basically trying to be a good little Christian and "speak every man the truth." They know this too and use your honesty against you by rending you with railing words about your disobedience being "as the sin of witchcraft" (I Samuel 15:23 taken out of context).

So why is it that the still small voice calling "danger Will Robinson, danger" is so easily ignored? After all this evidence how do they get away with it?

Partially because much of the behind-the-scenes training programs for the leaders are just that, behind-the-scenes, meaning they're secret and you rarely or never have an exposure to the truth of their training programs and the tactics they're taught. If you were able to get all the necessary behind-the-scenes information as you would with any university, you'd quickly see that most of the training is less to do with the Bible and more to do with obedience and control. They tell you your schedule, your work assignments, when to eat, even how to eat! Then on the field these leaders are expected to ply their trade on the ignorant but trusting followers, applying their "skills" with all their being. And all their controlling tactics begin lulling you into thinking the organization really is right so I must comply in order to please God and to remain in good standing with the "powers that be" in local leadership of the organization.

But it's more than just tactics of control. They also work at gaining trust by truly offering help in certain circumstances or by at least making you feel welcome in the early months of your involvement. At times they even also offer helpful advice like coaching expectant mothers on how to enter into labor without fear —no fear, no intense pain —and, oddly enough, such advice works. They'll even help you paint your house if you're recovering from surgery or preparing to move. So, between receiving genuine help and increasing suggestions, trust is won slowly over time, thus muting the voice calling "danger, danger".

The logic is balanced out even though sometimes the organization is tough and their expectations rather high. (Jesus was at times tough and He had lofty expectations of His disciples.) Plus they did lend genuine helping hands in areas where you perhaps hadn't received any before. The biblical doctrine they taught was plausible as well, so you decided to stick around, getting more committed in your studies and support of the organization.

Granted you haven't signed any contracts, other than the agreements for taking the classes, and you haven't consciously handed your life over to their hands. Nevertheless, the abdicating has begun. It's a funny thing how once commitment begins to set in, it brings with it guilt, guilt over not doing enough to prove your commitment or guilt for not bringing others along the same path you've chosen. After all, we are to reach the lost and you're no longer lost, right?

This could very well be the same psychology as when a person winds up being in a pretty bad intimate relationship. They cannot extricate themselves due to the guilt —especially if it has been a long time since experiencing romance. Now suddenly here's a new connection paying attention where no attention had been paid for a long time. Co-dependency is what this is called where each relationship feeds off the other for psychological support of fueling its own insecurities and ego. Granted this is an unhealthy relationship, since it centers on what the individual wants and needs rather than the love relationship Jesus promotes, where the motive is what can the individual give rather than take! In other words, a healthy relationship is one that seeks to fill the other's needs and not expect the other to fill all your needs —such relationships are doomed to failure even if they do still stay together.

Such as it is with cults, they feign that they offer you something —in this case, a "more than abundant life," but what they're really shooting for is another wallet and two more hands to do their work. They can't get you to stay with them if they don't somehow develop a relationship with you that will soon be ripe ground for cultivating guilt. Once they teach you their doctrine, which they of course refer to as truth, they can always use that against you if you choose not to live out their "truth." If this occurs, they "guilt" you back into conformity through one of the various tactics explained.

But, of course, this is never revealed to you so you instead believe the class will indeed teach you how to have power in your newly abundant life, and all this will be based on the Bible —what could go wrong? Again, such thought just further clears the way toward abdication. They promise to teach stuff you've always wanted to know and they'll do it with biblical principles, so sit back, relax, and let them drain your brain.

It first begins with the class. You sign a registration form actually requiring you to be on time for all twelve sessions plus the beginning orientation. Being on time to them means being ten minutes early —a particularly difficult thing for people like me who believe being on time is relative and five minutes on either side of being on time still counts as being on time —needless to say I nearly failed the class on this requirement alone. If you're late they threaten to kick you out of class whereby you forfeit the fees you paid since you didn't adhere to the agreement of being on time. You have to pay again if you wish to re-register for another class that may not take place for months and months.

Heaven forbid if you actually can't make a class session. In rare pre-arranged circumstances were people offered make-ups, but if no make-ups were arranged prior to the class beginning, you face being kicked out of the class if for some reason you didn't make a session. You weren't kicked out of their fellowships, of course, just the class. The fellowships are the places where they continue to indoctrinate you while also hopefully cajoling you into giving them money.

But what about traffic jams? Emergency overtime at work? Childcare issues or a sick child? Or if you got sick and were very contagious?

Nothing mattered, if you were late, you were dumped! If you didn't show, you were dumped, there was no grace, no compassion, you were just dumped. That was clue one, but being so new I was just excited to begin getting answers to my troubling questions that I complied with the timeframe without question, even though, as stated above, by nature I'm really a "just-in-time" sort of guy.

Another class requirement was laying aside all secular reading materials and reading only materials from the class: the syllabus of topics and Scripture references, and the actual books you got with the class, books written of course by the founder of the organization and the person who developed and taught the class. They encouraged you to turn aside all newspapers and magazines, any books you may be reading, and of course, anything of a theological nature.

I certainly understand adjusting a reading load based on what required reading there is for taking classes, but shunning all other reading material when you have time and a desire to read seems, as mentioned above, slightly extreme, even though much of the secular reading material isn't worth spending time with much less spending money on. Even so, cutting off all reading except material from the organization is very dangerous. For instance, you may wind up eliminating an opportunity to read something that could arrest your attention in such a way that you begin to hear very loudly the voice calling "danger."

Currently I'm reading a book I highly recommend called *The Best Question Ever* by Andy Stanley. I won't reveal what the question is but the book is so good I encourage you it buy it rather than borrow it. That way you can mark it up and write notes in it, or throw it against the wall only to retrieve it and keep reading through it. Now had I read something like it or even been exposed to something like it back in the mid-eighties, who knows where my walk with God would be now. However, since the organization encourages you, actually, requires you, to lay aside all other reading, this book would not have landed in my hands until after the class and after their talons had been sunk into the depths of my soul. Therefore, consider with great scrutiny any organization that urges you to lay aside all reading material except their own, and if you are urged to do so but choose not to, you may very well be thwarting a key strategy in building vulnerable in-roads into your thinking. This is called guarding you thinking and guarding your thinking is highly recommended by the Lord.

So you see how dangerous such a seemingly harmless requirement can be? Eliminate all other influences in your life and their indoctrination just becomes that much easier. They now have no interference into your cognitive processes, or put another way, your mind is open to just their input — dangerous, very dangerous.

And one last point I want to make on the class aspect. Since you have signed an "agreement" with them, they now use this document as an indication of your commitment to pursuing truth. Thus, they will use this sense of commitment as yet another avenue of inflicting guilt upon you should you begin to waver in attending or completing the class. They will press you to fulfill your commitment because that's what good, decent people do. They fulfill the commitments they make.

But, hey, let's face it, if we make a commitment to do something stupid, the right thing to do is break the commitment instead of doing something we know is stupid. Sure, we may wind up embarrassed for a while or even lose a friend or two through the process, but isn't that a better price to pay than years of wandering in the wilderness or completely wrecking our lives?

Who wouldn't end an engagement to the fiancé who turned out to be a lying floozy rather than the pure chess player you thought she was? Or what about that nice guy with the good job and great benefits who was also a compulsive gambler with insurmountable debts and spotty employment record? Or the potential child-care provider who you found out has a record of sexual misconduct.

In other words, if you've made a commitment that winds up not being what you thought it was, feel free to break it off, to flee far from it, to throw the baby and the bathwater out the window. If they try pressing you with guilt about breaking a commitment, just politely mention that they mislead you into making the decision in the first place. In doing this you clearly point out to them that it is they who are breaking commitments by shrouding the truth of who they really are. Chances are they won't receive this well, but you can at least feel assured that you are doing the right thing regardless of what they say or do.

But if the commitment is kept, then with these rules in place and with your adherence to them you are now being primed for abdication. For by agreeing to the precepts of the class, you are also adjusting who you are for who they want you to become. You are unconsciously shifting your identity from yourself, from your internal view of who you think you are and should be, over to them and who they think you should be. This is also very dangerous because God has purposed each of us and who He wants us to become, our identity really rests in Him, so as the cult tries to change that, your world begins to fall apart.

CHAPTER SIXTEEN

How Bad Can it Be?

——+——

"This is too warm work, Hardy, to last long."
—Lord Horatio Nelson to his friend and
Naval captain, Thomas Hardy,
at the beginning of what turned
out to be a very long battle, the
Battle of Trafalgar, and shortly
before he was mortally wounded.

"Of man's first disobedience, and the fruit Of that
forbidden tree whose mortal taste Brought death into
the world, and all our woe."
—John Milton, from Paradise Lost

In the early afternoon of October of 21st 1805, a confident Admiral Nelson commanding the British Fleet was about to engage the Combined Fleet of French and Spanish ships in the epoch sea battle known as the Battle of Trafalgar. He intended to enter into the battle with an unconventional tactic dubbed the "Nelson's Touch." Historians suggest that Admiral Nelson had expected the French to set sail and run instead of doing what they did, standing up to the attack and fighting back. Ultimately, of course, Admiral Nelson's fleet defeated the Combined Fleet even though the admiral himself had been shot after a little more than an hour of a battle that waged all day long. Even though dying before the battle's conclusion, he was a hero of mega-celebrity status, almost deified among the thronging masses back home.

Okay, yes, I'm a nautical history buff and I know you're probably thinking what does this battle have to do with cults? On the surface, pardon the pun, nothing. However, some comparisons do bear note.

I know this is a bit of a stretch but let's say the family of believers are the British Fleet, each ship is a church or other genuine Christ-following organization, and you and I are crew on one of the ships. And let's say our enemy, the devil and his minions, are the Combined Fleet. Our Admiral, Jesus Christ, also sacrificed His life on our behalf in the waging battle. However, in our battle, just like at Trafalgar, there are and will continue to be many casualties because our enemy is not intending on setting sail and running. He is standing his ground and fighting. The "Nelson's Touch" in our battle is a combination of Jesus' resurrection from the dead and His Great Commission to His church of spreading the gospel —the good news of salvation —throughout the world.

And like the British Fleet, Jesus' "fleet" will eventually be successful but not without a continued price. In the Battle of Trafalgar over 8,000 lives were lost and many more were permanently maimed or scarred in some way. Also several ships were sunk and many more were completely disabled, becoming nothing more than floating hulks of shot up wood and blood. This is the goal of the enemy in our battle, to maim if not kill believers and seekers, and to eventually sink as many ships as possible. Cults operate as enemy ships, sailing about seeking easy targets to riddle with cannon shot, maiming and scarring people to such a degree that they never seek after Christ again, or become so fooled they actually join the devil's fleet.

While the Bible promises that as we resist the devil, he will flee (see James 4:7b), we don't know how long it will take for him to flee nor how long he will remain "fleed." In other words, even though his destiny is sealed as we read in the Book of Revelation, the Bible also says that up until his defeat, he continues striving toward stealing, killing, and destroying (see John 10:10a) and seeking whom he may devour (see I Peter 5:8). The Bible also refers to the devil as an "ancient serpent" (see Revelation 12:9 and 20:2), and since he's ancient you can bet he's learned several tricks along the way, tricks to fool us and to trap us in webs of deceit we can hardly recognize much less escape from. Such are the aspects of warfare. The victims in this warfare, however, are not volunteer sailors or conscripted vagabonds, but families with children, families whose parents desired to find the Lord to avoid damnation and ruin and to teach their children the right way to go.

But since the devil is ancient and crafty, many fall instead into the trap of the cult, into the trap of "we have something even better to offer than the churches," something that at the outset sounds more genuine but is really nothing more than a thin veneer hiding the sweltering pit of darkness underneath.

In the previous chapters I've attempted to isolate various tactics of control on more universal levels and how our desires for meaning and significance influence and foster our vulnerabilities for belonging. In this chapter I would like to share a few poignant yet painful examples of how the abdication invaded my home, contributing to the destruction of my marriage and damaging the psyche of all those pelted in one way or another by the debris of disaster. When lives fall apart, the destruction is great and far-reaching, even to reaching beyond the specific generation that got into the mess to begin with.

On yet another evening the phone rang again. Yep, you guessed it, it was Tracey.

"Craig, we have an important leader's meeting tomorrow morning in Portland."

"Okay," I replied obediently. "When and where do I need to be?"

"It's so important, Craig, that you both need to be there."

I took a deep breath. Had she forgotten that we have a young son? Finding a babysitter in less than twelve hours was not going to be easy.

"Well okay, I think Nellie should stay home with our son, but I can sure go and ..."

"No, Craig, you both need to be there. That's been made very clear to me. Just find a babysitter. In fact," she paused, "call me later tonight about your effort to find a babysitter. Just believe God."

That was that. It seemed the answer for everything was to just believe God. Obviously since ministry leadership deemed it necessary for both of us to be at the meeting all we had to do was to believe big enough to find a baby sitter. They were convinced that since they decided to have a meeting it was now all of the sudden God's will. Funny, I didn't think God's will was so easy to control —just decide what you want, then state it's the will of God; how convenient.

And is God's will really so poorly planned? Isn't the Creator of the entire universe just a little more organized than that? It was incredible to me how such poor planning on their part was now my problem to solve. Why didn't they believe God to be better planners of meetings that required not only travel but child care arrangements as well. Now I was stuck in a tough spot between my family and my leadership responsibilities, and to top it off I had to talk to her again tonight.

Tracey always made my stomach hurt and she was the last person on the face of the planet that I wanted to talk to.

As time went on that waning Friday evening, I found no one who could baby-sit. One Grandma was involved in a church ministry that she coordinated, and the other Grandma was taking care of a disabled grandchild. Our friends couldn't do it either, so we were left with no one to care for our three-year-old son.

With great hesitancy I called Tracey back and told her the news for which my solution was for Nellie to stay home. After all, being a Mom was a much more important responsibility than any meeting planned at the last minute.

"No," she shot back. "I have a day care contact where you drop your son off tomorrow morning. She takes emergency drop-ins."

"What? But I don't even know who she is. How can I trust her?"

"Because I've left my daughter with her once and she was just fine. Now, write down this address."

And on the conversation went. I'm sure as you read this you're thinking what I'm thinking as I write it: what was I thinking? A whole ton of "should haves" comes flooding in. I should have told Tracey to take a hike. I should have told her what I thought of their last minute meetings. I should have let her know she has no authority over my home and who in my home goes to what meetings. I should have told her that without proper interviews and inspections my son will only stay with us or other trusted friends or family. I should have ... well, you get the point.

But cowardly, I complied. What a forfeiture of parental authority. What a caving in of fatherly oversight. What a watered down wimp. This was a huge step in abdicating the spiritual authority over my home. Here I should have taken a stand to protect my son and to defend the role of his mother to stay with her priority responsibility of caring for our child over going to a last-minute meeting. Instead, under a black cloud of guilt and self-condemnation, we dropped our son off at a day care provider we had never met before. Just think of the horrors that could have happened. Talk about sheer stupidity of following orders of a woman I didn't like nor thought was the brightest star in the sky, but who still insisted I drop my one and only son (at that time, anyway) off with total strangers with a bunch of total stranger kids.

I look back on it now viewing it as sheer insanity.

But somehow God still protected our son.

By the time the day was over, our son was fine but there was an unspoken division between my wife and me. How could I have let this happen? Why didn't I take a stand like any other dad? Where was my backbone?

Good question. Even though I didn't make that mistake again I had lost valuable relational ground in my marriage that was never regained. Granted, there were more problems in my marriage than just that, and many of the problems were not associated with me, but owning my problems has helped me from repeating the same mistakes and will also hopefully help you not make the same mistakes as well.

As stated earlier, my biggest problem was spiritual abdication. Allowing my self and my family to be bullied by an organization with poor planning and no regard for the well being of my family is abdication squared. This occurred several years ago and to this day I still vividly remember the aspects regarding my son, but cannot recall a shred of memory of what that meeting was about. Imagine, a nondescript meeting could have been a catalyst for permanent damage had God not protected the well-being of our son.

For you time management fans, meetings are never a higher priority than the safety and security of your family. And if they are, you may want to really check out why your family is prioritized lower than a meeting that will most likely be forgotten within the week.

In light of the metaphor at the beginning of this chapter, I wasn't on a ship of a mainstream church and I was certainly not fully on board the organization's ship either, but instead I was merely on a little skiff, nothing more than a rickety old lifeboat, scudding over very rough seas while the ship looming over my bow was that of the organization. Quickly it set sails to bear down on me, raking my upper decks, that is my thought processes, with obliterating grape shot of demands and expectations, slicing into pieces all in its path. It reduced my thinking to Jell-o, nothing more than a moldable ooze they could shape for their own purposes.

No organization, perhaps not even employers, should ever be allowed to force a person to place their own family in peril. This seems so obvious now, but when an organization has worked hard to convince you they represent God, then the obvious becomes obscured by their rhetoric and conditioning and all the black and white issues of life are blurred into a whirling gray, like being caught at sea in a fog bank that slithered up quietly and quickly. Only the most adept at navigation will successfully avoid grounding or hitting the shallow shoals looming off most coasts, but the rest of us run headlong into the rocks, shattering the fragile bows of our lives, and taking on water at an alarming rate!

Another such example that just added to the water rushing into the once watertight holds of our lives was Tracey again inserting herself into the private life of my wife.

Again, perhaps more accurately rendered, she was **allowed** to insert herself into our lives. She could have been staved off at the gate so-to-speak had I employed one or more of the "should haves" mentioned earlier, but, alas, I didn't, because the black and white issues of life were obscured in the whirling gray of swirling indistinguishable blobs of right and wrong —which blobs were truth and which blobs were lies —I couldn't tell in the confusion. I reluctantly relented to my so-called leader.

This was the encounter alluded to in Chapter Ten. Nellie and I were summoned to the back room for yet another chat. In tow was our son fast asleep in his carrier. Tracey had made her daughter leave her room, since that's where the meeting was, and go into her mom's room to fall asleep. Why we couldn't have gone into mom's room instead of disrupting a little girl's sleep, I don't know.

At this point, Tracey dug in.

She spent the better part of an hour and a half explaining how Nellie was failing as a believer and thus as a wife and mother. How she knew this without actually living with Nellie was never revealed, but she insisted she could figure this out through conversations with Nellie and with other friends of Nellie's from the fellowship. Looking back on this it sounds more like spies trying to sabotage a person they didn't like or were jealous of, but at the heat of the discussion, our brains were mush and we didn't float this thought out as a counter to her searing and unfounded accusations.

So there we sat, being pounded for ninety minutes. The bottom line of all the grilling was that Nellie didn't spend enough time with God in prayer or in reading His Word and the accompanying ministry materials. Basically, Nellie wasn't like Tracey and Tracey was the model for the women in our fellowship to aspire to.

Several things are wrong with this, not least of which is God made each of us unique according to His purposes for our lives (see Psalm 139). None of us will ever be a carbon copy of another and God doesn't expect this either. Rather, God expects us to enter into deeper relationship with Him according to how He designed us, not how society or some organization conditioned us or is trying to condition us. Be wary of any group trying to corral the human spirit into a vanilla blend of blandness and uniformity. Their bottom line in doing this is really to snuff out individuality so as to program the masses into complying with their wishes. Remove uniqueness from the individual then you can control that emptied individual with your programming and direction. Once emptied of the essence of who you are, you then dote about trying to fill that empty void, and those responsible for the emptying process are more than happy to fill your void with their rhetoric and commands. Look at all the world's most notorious dictators from Stalin to Pol Pat to Hitler and you'll see on a much grander scale the same tactics most cults employ —destroy individuality then program the empty receptacles of once vibrant human souls with your own nefarious directives.

This is not to be confused with Philippians 2 where we are called to empty ourselves of our egos to instead put on the mind of Christ. As we will later see, Christ works in peaceable and gentle ways, honoring our uniqueness and endeavoring to foster and augment that uniqueness. If anything comes along that is trying to vanquish your uniqueness, it is highly likely it is not from Jesus. Therefore as you sense someone trying to mold you into their image rather than into the image of Christ, flee!

But again, I didn't grasp any of this so many years ago.

So even though we had all the means of escape at our disposal by just saying 'no', we perceived our situation as having no choice but to endure and obey.

Tracey put together a plan she wanted Nellie to adhere to and that she expected me to oversee to assure Nellie did indeed adhere to it. Then she put together a "reporting back" arrangement so that Tracey could have the eventual end-say in the progress Nellie was making or not making. She was required to report via email on a weekly basis on her progress of adhering to the "Tracey directives." These involved a daily reading schedule and getting in touch with the other women in our fellowship group on a regular basis either via phone of meeting for coffee or lunch. Perhaps this sounds a bit harmless but a weekly email reporting your past week's efforts is to me quite intrusive. And gathering with other women in the fellowship may sound like a means for deepening friendships except Nellie had nothing in common with these women plus the organization had so brow-beat them in the past that when they did meet for their private conversations, everyone was so careful of what they were saying that no one really opened their heart to anything. Why? Well, mostly because if someone said something out of line the other person would invariably report that back to Tracey, precipitating yet more back room chats and more intrusive mechanisms for correction. So, what the organization effectively did was program its people to be nothing more than surface-level, legalistic religious boobs; no one genuinely shared the deeper things of the heart which ultimately meant the deep hurts of our lives were buried even deeper almost assuring deliverance would never occur without exiting the organization itself.

There were also other aspects never taken into consideration. Tracey was of robust health and seemed very driven. Nellie, while wanting to be committed to her beliefs, had health conditions affecting her abilities to concentrate as well as other areas of her life. Mentioned earlier was her diagnosed condition of fybromyalgia. Coupled with this but diagnosed at a much later time after exiting the organization and the divorce was a condition of Level 2 Bi-polar. These dual conditions wreaked havoc on many areas of Nellie's life, not to mention the difficulties it brought to our marriage.

But the organization frowned on psychiatry of any kind, including psychiatric drugs. Thankfully Nellie and I didn't subscribe to this thinking and she was able to begin some treatment with psychiatric drugs, but this process itself can be very difficult until doctors begin to really hone in on which drugs are actually needed. Until they get to this point, personalities can be so badly effected that all kinds of troubles occur. This is a topic best suited for psychology professionals, but a great source for understanding more deeply brain chemical imbalances is *Blue Genes* by Dr. Paul Meier. In this book he explains in detail how brain chemical imbalances are no different than any other physiological problem of genetics like diabetes or high blood pressure. For some reason our culture is more accepting of physiological problems with any other organ except the brain. When the brain is affected we label that as a mental health issue which usually receives the stigma of a person being crazy or lazy or some other denigrating stigma.

The organization was no different. They would even go to the length of insinuating that mental health issues were more demonic possession than anything else. Funny, medical research and scientific studies do not corroborate such labeling.

Even so, the stigma of the organization made it very hard for us to tell them the problems because they refused to accept them and only espoused what they always espoused, believe God to get over it. Well, it never occurred to anyone that perhaps God, who knew us before the womb, allowed the conditions but had enablements at our disposal to combat those conditions[16] , or, to accept those conditions using them for His glory. Maybe we're not meant to get rid of these conditions but are instead called to seek God more deeply so He can use us, conditions and all, to reach people who otherwise might not be reached. Maybe our conditions will help us reach people with the same or similar conditions that the rest of society shuns or just flat can't deal with.

But this organization never saw things that way. They believed all people should be of perfect health, even though the founder of the organization eventually died of cancer.

So, through this time of not allowing the individual to be an individual we desperately tried to comply to the wishes of the organization. In doing so, I never said enough was enough and we struggled as a couple at the impossible task of being people who we weren't. The damage of trying to be who we weren't drove insurmountable fissures between us that eventually lead to infidelity and finally, to divorce court. And through all of this was a little boy watching as the very security he had known all his short life crumbled to the ground in heaps of tears and sorrows, never to be resurrected again.

So how bad can it be? That bad! Bad enough to bring a marriage to destruction. Bad enough to cause irreparable damage to the psyche of the most innocent of all —children.

There are other examples of intrusive control. Examples such as judging Nellie by a pair of shoes the leader thought were inappropriate. The leader thought Nellie's shoes looked "witchy" and therefore shouldn't be worn; never mind the fact the shoes were stylish and looked good on her. Or the very tight control over how the fellowship group prepared for the whole Y2K flop, all the way down to taking inventories of stored water (which, of course, goes bad very quickly), mobile communications, and food storage. Then there were the events we were supposed to figure out how to get to, events that occurred thousands of miles away that required time off of work, travel, and accommodations at great expense.

I remember one time we went to the annual festival called the Rock of Ages. A hurricane had ripped through the gulf coasts the week prior and remnants of the storm continued north, even as far as Ohio where the festival was. Well, we pitched our little tent where we were told to but low and behold, with the pelting rains and the soggy, swamp-like pasture ground we had to pitch our tent in, it flooded, endangering not just our stuff, but our thirteen-month-old son. Well, thankfully God provided a nearby hotel room but I still got the third-degree lecture for not ensuring my tent was waterproof. I did, of course, check for that before we left Oregon but who knew we'd be camped in high winds and torrential rains of a spinning out hurricane? And why did the organization insist on us having to camp in an already over-saturated pasture? They did finally provide us with emergency shelter, but not until after we had a harrowing experience of trying to save our belongings while also protecting our son. All this could have been avoided had the organization closed off the saturated pastures and provided the shelter at the beginning.

There are, of course, even more examples of abdication, but these are the most telling if not painful to present. Hopefully the examples give fodder for you and others of what to watch out for in groups of people or specific leaders as well.

But what about biblical ammunition? What Scripture can we arm ourselves with for such situations? Here are some examples.

James 3:17 says "but the wisdom that comes from heaven is first of all pure; then peace loving, considerate, submissive, full of mercy, and good fruit, impartial and sincere (NIV)." The King James Version of this verse says this wisdom is "peaceable, gentle, and easy to be entreated." The New American Standard Bible says "peaceable, gentle, reasonable."

Do you see a theme here? In all that was described in this chapter, nothing brought peace to our souls. In fact, just the opposite, it brought turmoil, conflict, and disunity. There was no gentleness at all. It was commands and unilaterally established expectations. It wasn't easy to be entreated, that is, easy to accept or abide by. It was instead disruptive and intrusive. And it was completely unreasonable. Nowhere were there multilateral discussions, or consideration of health conditions, or any thought of considering that the observations that were seen may have been through biased eyes rather than viewing the whole picture. No, it was a series of unreasonable expectations and unreasonable intrusion on our private lives.

Thus, as ideas or expectations get thrown at you, send them through the filter of James 3:17. If they don't stand muster through that filter, they're most likely not from God.

Another verse of Scripture that is a great filter is Colossians 3:15, "let the peace of Christ rule in your hearts, since as members of one body you were called to peace. And be thankful (NIV)."

The influence of Christ is to bring peace to our souls rather than bitterness or quarrelsomeness. Likewise, belonging to the body of Christ should be a peaceful experience rather than a painful one. If there's bitterness or pain in orders or commands being placed upon you, again, it's likely not from God and therefore worthy of being shunned. If an organization or person consistently violates the screens of these two verses, they ought to be examined closely for what they really are and what their true motives may be. They could just be inexperienced and clumsy, or, more than likely, they are entering into cult-like tendencies if not developing into a full-blown cult.

With such navigational understanding and Scriptural screening, you will be able to land safely on a ship in the right fleet heading in the right direction and avoid being a casualty yourself in the spiritual warfare that continually wages unseen around us every day.

CHAPTER SEVENTEEN

Underbelly and Prejudice

—+—

"When will I ever learn?"
        —Snoopy, after crashing while jump roping.

"The truth will set you free."
                                                —Jesus, John 8:32b.

It was a Wednesday as I recall, moving day. The day was warm and sunny, expected high in the eighties with no chance of rain, a typical July summer day in the Willamette Valley. But today was moving day. I gathered my son as we grabbed our sack lunches and beach toys, piled into the cab of my red S-10 and drove away, it was moving day, you see. The day my wife and her new friend would back a big old rental truck into our driveway to empty the house of what was deemed hers —furniture, dishes, clothes, and memories, wonderful and horrible alike. I was taking my son to the coast, my favorite place on earth, so he wouldn't have to see the spectacle of separation, the dismantling of dreams, and the humiliation of failure. And so I could somehow find some solace in the ever-present majesty of the ocean. It felt like my life was spinning out of control, like a pulsar spinning at 30 times a second!

The sense of desperation in my heart was so deep and thick that I literally felt I was hauling bricks attached to the lower lobes of my lungs. My breathing was labored and my heart wouldn't stop palpitating, it palpitated so hard at night the bed literally vibrated from the thumping in my chest. There were times I thought for sure my carotid was going to explode then and there, thankfully ending this cruel season of life but then leaving my son in a totally empty house. I'm no Job, but I couldn't imagine things getting much worse.

"What had gone wrong?" I thought to myself. "What are we going to do now?" "How can I pay for a lawyer?" "Where's God?" "How's my son going to deal with this?" "How could this happen to us?"

These and other questions pounded on my consciousness like a fire hose on a protestor.

Granted, the cult wasn't the sole reason for the divorce. There were other factors not related to me or the cult, but for my part of the divorce, how would things have been different had I not been so inculcated with the organization's doctrine, or their cold-heartedness to physical and mental health issues? Or if we had a real relationship with Jesus rather than an arms-length, let's-put-Jesus-in-our-box kind of approach with Him?

Who knows? No one, of course, and to continue dwelling in so many "what ifs" only lengthens the healing and deepens the bitterness. But thank God and hallelujah! Those days are over!

Ironically, though, at this exact moment in my life, I didn't really have friends other than the ones in the organization. Talk about spinning out of control!

When my son and I returned to the house, it was very empty in certain rooms, particularly my room. All that was left were piles of clothes on the floor, no bed, no dresser, nothing. I had to sleep in my son's upper bunk until I got a bed for myself. We didn't know where his mother was going to go but she would contact us when she could. Thankfully, we agreed our son would stay with me because, as she said herself, she "wanted him raised in the Word of God" and she said "I know you'll do that." Even she was still fooled at this stage.

But this statement revealed much. Even though our marriage was over and she was moving out, she still saw me and my commitment to the organization as the godly thing to do and wanted our son raised in a godly environment. It's funny, even after all the abuse heaped upon us and the resulting fraying and ultimate failure of our marriage, we both still clung to the organization like the bleeding woman reaching for the hem of Jesus' garment.

Remember how earlier I stated that cults prey on middle-class people who are disillusioned with the church but still want to seek after God? Prime example right here. After all these years and all the abuses already mentioned, we were still thinking we were where God wanted us. Deceptions of darkness run deep, even in those of godly intent.

While the next two weeks of just my son and I were rough, people in the organization were there to help, and they were literally real helpful to me though still keeping a close eye on me.

As time went on and the ugly legal details of divorce were being completed, I moved deeper into leadership in the organization. Why, you ask? Because I had nowhere else to go and I felt significant, like I had a purpose, like I was still able to fill needs of others while being pleasing to God. Plus, I didn't want to be any more alone than I already was. Life can be pretty dreary at three-o-clock in the morning when you wake up alone, with nothing but darkness and shattered dreams.

How easily I forgot that not even a year ago my wife and I were being mercilessly harassed by a pseudo-leader that worshipped the organization and its tenants but cared little for my family and me and was clueless to the damage she was causing to the fabric of life under our roof. By this time, that particular leader had moved on and left in her place her favorite couple to replace her. Thankfully this couple had a little more compassion for people, but still liked riding my butt on many details that were really none of their business. He was a no-nonsense former party-animal and she was thoughtful and laid back. Together they had built a home-based window cleaning business into a huge success and had potential for even bigger and better enterprises. What they did instead, though, was dedicate more and more of their life into the organization, even to the point of selling their business and joining the Corps program mentioned in earlier chapters. They had so much potential for business, for a family, or even for the true God that it is a shame to think of all that gifting going into the support of an organization that specializes in minimizing Jesus while racking and ruining innocent but desperate lives. I have since lost touch with them and don't know if they finished their training or not, but they were definitely the kind of dynamos the organization wanted and needed for continued survival.

In time I became their assistant fellowship leader since I had to let go of my group during the divorce. I learned a lot from them even though I'm a lot older, but I was still never able to be quite myself around them. They, too, had the knack for correcting everything I said and they even employed similar tactics of confrontation as Tracey, particularly the "call people over to your house for a meeting but not tell them why" trick. I saw this pulled on a burly guy who had gotten a tattoo without their permission. Had he sought their advice they would have told him it was unbiblical and that he shouldn't do it. But instead of just talking to him about their opinion, they called him over to their house to join them and me. Yes, I was dragged in on this, and the confrontation began. I did try to get them to consider a different approach but that was what they were taught and that's what they did, especially since they knew he would be caught off guard and thus not be prepared for a counter argument. He would, in essence, be ambushed just as we were, and then subjected to their pounding lecture of condemnation and how they viewed his behavior as disobedience. This guy was also one of their employees so he was soon to be put into a very uncomfortable spot —having his "spiritual" leaders and employers confront him.

So here I was on the other side of the table, which was almost as uncomfortable as being on the side of the confronted. The only redeeming thing about this episode was the beginning of viewing the ugly underbelly of the organization. My suspicions were now beginning to prove themselves as not wicked thoughts against God's people or God's ministry, but instead as an affirmation that the suspicions were honest analysis and godly warnings. The bottom line truth of it all was they hurt people; certainly something Jesus would never command nor condone.

But as time went on and they prepared to leave the state, I took the leadership again of the fellowship. Now I was in a position to get even more first-hand glimpses of the uglier underbelly of the organization since now I was reporting to the highest leader in the state rather than to one of his subordinates as I had before.

As we delve further into this chapter, I really want to repeat that I am not intending this work to be a trashy kiss-and-tell exploit of innocent people. However, I am endeavoring to give real-life examples illustrating tactics and motives that will hopefully help you steer clear of such organizations. Hopefully it will also help churches, church leaders, and general Christ-followers from falling into the same patterns or tactics that cults employ. In other words, hopefully exposure to these issues and situations will assist in keeping one's walk with the Lord genuine instead of tainted with works-oriented, compassionless hypocrisy.

If you spend any time at all with people who have rejected Christ or at least who have rejected the "organized church," you will most likely find at the core of the rejection an experience where they were hurt, lied to, or otherwise greatly offended by someone calling themselves "Christian." Stated another way, it is often so-called Christians themselves who cause the most damage to the advancement of Christ's Kingdom. In this work are prime examples of that as well as other behavioral traps set cunningly by the adversary himself, the devil, that are set for us to easily fall into. Let's face it, it's easy to become automatic with people who have problems or who are somewhat hostile to our faith, but the Spirit of the Lord continually leads us to be compassionate to the hurting and patient with the angry.

The fellowship that I led had, of course, a number of broken people in it. But whether we admit it or not, we're all broken and Jesus was sent to heal the broken (see Isaiah 61 and Luke 4). So this was, if it were a traditional church-connected small group, perfect ground to see the Lord work in an up close and personal way. Obviously, though, this was not a group connected to a Christ-following church, but instead a group connected to a cult with its main leaders three thousand miles away. Their link to my fellowship was by way of their main leader in Oregon who was sent from headquarters. We'll call him Joe.

Joe was a good schmoozer and could really talk well about almost anything. Not particularly educated, he was articulate and fun to be around — most of the time.

But one summer evening while I was sitting at my dining room table with pen and tablet ready, I waited by the phone for his weekly call (he lived fifty miles away so we communicated via phone and email until our monthly meetings or he came to visit). The conversation was pretty much business as usual until we landed on his desire to know about details of the people in my fellowship.

Curt, not his real name of course, was a diabetic, and his particular type of diabetes was very debilitating, so much so that his endocrinologist was recommending he get hooked up to an insulin pump. Most people can manage their diabetes through insulin injections, diet, and exercise. Usually this regimen is successful in assisting balance and a relatively normal life. Some people, however, as I understand it anyway, can have such huge blood sugar swings that sleeping can become dangerous. They're sound asleep, their blood sugar plummets, and they wind up in insulin shock, or diabetic coma, or even die. Not a pretty thing for the diabetic or their spouse. To counter this potential, medical science has developed an insulin pump that regulates and administers insulin when needed. Pretty sweet deal if you ask me. But not if you ask Joe.

So that particular summer evening with a clear sky, dazzling sunset, birds singing and frogs and crickets croaking and chirping, I was suddenly immersed into a caldron of darkness.

I told Joe that Curt and his wife had successfully believed God for the wherewithal to secure an insulin pump.

"He doesn't need an insulin pump," Joe blurted into the phone.

"Well, yes he does," I stammered. "He has such a serious case of diabetes that his doctor highly recommended he get such a pump. It could save his life."

"Ha, he's just lazy. He won't take care of himself like a normal disciplined person, lazy, that's all it is."

"Lazy? He's diabetic."

"Craig, even Proverbs says the sluggard is too lazy to feed himself, Curt's just lazy."

How could that be, I thought to myself, I've seen Curt work very hard on various projects over the years. Was I hearing true spiritual discernment or pompous prejudice based in ignorance? Joe had a strong tendency to state his opinions as if they were facts that should end the conversation right there. To attempt to continue with conversation was to expose myself to more closed-door confrontations since I was obviously not being humble to my leader and his wisdom as God worked in his soul (perhaps it's more like god —with lowercase 'g' —that was working in his soul). But I couldn't let this one go. My Dad had diabetes, not this bad, but he had it so I had some knowledge about the condition and to watch for it creeping up in my life as well. Therefore, I could tell Joe didn't know squat about it. So I pressed on even though he had just sounded one of many pronouncing opinions of his perception of facts.

"I don't think he's lazy, Joe, I think he's sick and working hard to get well."

He didn't pause for even a second to consider what I had just said. "Well Craig," he said, "you can think what you want, but I discern he's just lazy." That's what Tracey said about my ex-wife, that Nellie didn't have fibromyalgia, she was just lazy, just making up excuses so she didn't have to do any work. Hmm, must be a theme corps people are taught. If there's something wrong with someone in your fellowship that you don't understand, that must mean they're lazy. In my book that isn't discernment. It's just ignorance and prejudice that eventually results in shaming the person who is legitimately suffering from an illness that they neither asked for nor can get rid of. And who's really lazy here, the person suffering from some ailing condition or the person unwilling to actually gather information and learn more about the ailment. Seems the latter is lazier than the former. And how are we to read Psalm 34:5 stating that "those who look to him are radiant; their faces are never covered with shame?" I would definitely conclude that any organization or leader fostering shame in the people they lead is not sent from the true God and definitely does not represent Jesus.

Another warning to Christ-followers is if you or your church rhetoric centers around statements or sermons of guilt and shame, don't be surprised to someday find yourself with no one around you. Why would God respond to desperate seekers by sending them to someone who was just going to exponentially increase the guilt and shame they so desire to be released from? He's not, plain and simple. That's why ministries, and even churches, whither on the vine. They've succumbed to a scheme of the enemy that has now rendered them ineffective to advancing the Kingdom of God.

Okay, back to Joe. I could see the thick wall of personal opinion surrounding Joe's brain was impenetrable on this issue. So we ventured on to the next person, although I knew that since I had dared challenge his opinion I was now slowly beginning to lose favor with him. That is, I was slowly getting myself on his list of people to keep an eye on.

"How's Doris," he asked.

I could hardly wait to answer this one. Doris was an eighty-five year old widow, a devout follower of the organization who had lost both legs below the knee because of circulation problems stemming from progressive worsening of, yep, you guessed it, diabetes. She'd also had a stroke at one point in her life and had open-heart surgery at another point; so health-wise, she was mess. She took several prescription medicines and had umpteen doctor appointments throughout the year. In her younger years, she was married to an abusive alcoholic and worked long hard weeks in the casinos of Las Vegas. She was now living with her "unbeliever sister" some sixty miles away, but she still diligently drove herself to my home so she could hear God's Word, even though she had to maneuver her walker up a small flight of stairs to get into my living room. Cult or not, this was one woman worthy of great admiration. She was committed, she persevered through tons of adversity, and she was always cheerful and full of joy. What a lady! She loved to tell stories of God's goodness and give advice on how to cope with and move through adversity.

"Well, Joe, she's completely debt-free now and ready to register for the Advanced Class." As stated earlier, this was the class the organization considered their premiere class of spiritual insight. Anybody who was anybody needed to take this class.

"I dunno, Craig. She's so old and frail that she'd need a lot of help that headquarters probably couldn't give her."

My jaw hit the floor. I couldn't believe what I just heard. Here's one of the most committed folks I know, who had over the years given thousands of dollars in tithes to this organization so people like him could draw a salary and now he was actually saying they would refuse her access to the class they consider the only class of it's caliber in the world? What was he thinking? Man oh man, talk about a double-whammy of discrimination. She's not only disabled, she's elderly as well. If only I were a lawyer!

"I'm sorry, Joe, I didn't quite get that." I was really thinking about the absurdity of his statement, but knew better than to say so, so I stalled.

"She has a walker, takes a lot of medicine, needs a special diet, would need help getting around the campus. I think she'd require more attention than headquarters could give her."

Here's my translation of his intent. She's too old to make an impact in recruiting so why should we put any effort into her? Let her live her life out as an Intermediate class grad instead.

Don't dictators ration based upon usefulness to the "cause" rather than the value of human life? Didn't Jesus teach about finding that one lost sheep, even though ninety-nine were already accounted for? Hadn't this woman's tithe offerings helped to fund the making of this class?

"Are you sure, Joe?" I was really on thin ice with him now. Here was a second opinion of his I was questioning.

"Yes, Craig, I am. I'll think about it, but I'm pretty sure that's how it needs to be handled."

I'm sure old hard-nosed Joe would have had me break the news to her to, but thankfully I left the organization before that day came.

Onto the next person. Rather than bore you with more detail, I'll summarize the opinions regarding the next folks.

There was a single woman in my fellowship with two children. The boy was in early high school and the girl was in middle school. Her boy was not the least bit athletic but preferred, instead, all things electronic. The kid had a great mind for the electronics and for science fiction, especially Star Trek. He was a nice kid, though not particularly social, but still a nice kid and quite intelligent just the same. Joe's opinion of him? He was effeminate. Why? Because any "normal" boy his age would be out playing baseball —just like he did —instead of hanging out indoors dinking around with a computer screen.

A family of four was also in my fellowship. The wife struggled with depression and had actually been prescribed a psychiatric drug to help balance her out by adjusting brain chemicals. While she wasn't necessarily considered lazy, she was considered weak. Why? Because, according to Joe, all she needed to do was just make up her mind not be depressed, and then, I guess, bang, instant cure! Funny, I'm sure, like most depressed people, if they could stop it themselves they would. But unfortunately brain chemical imbalances don't just fix themselves because you want them to, just like high blood pressure often doesn't lower simply because you want it to. No matter how much you exercise or eat right, outside help is needed. Truth be told, though, she was the most compassionate and caring person in the whole lot. She had a genuine kindness that was readily apparent to all she met, even when she was forced to go door-to-door witnessing. However, she was stuck in a marriage that was cult-influenced and therefore drove on an autocratic autopilot. Her husband was, while on the surface nice and helpful, actually very controlling. His home ran on schedule (kind of like the father in Mary Poppins), his children were unusually subdued for their ages, sickness was weakness, and every ministry event had to be attended regardless of effort, cost, or impact on the family. What was Joe's opinion of him? A prime example of discipline and commitment, an example we should all aspire to. It also didn't hurt that he made a significant salary and tithed a lot to the organization! He was always an example of financial management since he owned his home outright. Only what wasn't mentioned, however, was that to get to that point his parents had given him a substantial sum of money to buy his first home fifteen years or so earlier. Had we all been given such resources perhaps more of us would own our homes outright as well.

He was also the little spy in my fellowship that I later discovered was reporting to Joe about my various doings, especially since I had started exhibiting a propensity for questioning Joe's opinions, which in his mind, was akin to questioning authority, thus, rebellion. Plus, it seems that even though I was a fellowship leader, I was still different enough from everyone else to warrant suspicion, partially because I did question Joe, but also because I still had a streak of freedom in my soul. In a very real way, this husband and I were polar opposites, even though we were in the same organization, we were very different personalities. I would push the envelope from time to time while he would unquestioningly adhere to all directives coming from either headquarter or from Joe. He's the consummate agent of leadership, blindly obedient to their edicts and commands while I was desiring to be obedient but still sometimes questioning tactic and motive. I was, after all, raised by a defense attorney.

Through this process of divorce and the discovery of ugliness and prejudice, the old independent Craig was beginning to return. I was again returning to the roots of seeking truth rather than blindly adhering to precepts that seemed based in circumstances and not in truth.

Perhaps the spirit of Christ housed in my soul wasn't completely dormant after all.

CHAPTER EIGHTEEN

The Beginning of the End

—+—

"Be not unequally yoked together with unbelievers."
-II Corinthians 6:14 (KJV).

*D*eception is often like the art or effort of seduction — the seduced doesn't realize they're being reeled into a cunning trap, set only for the advantage of the trapper but never for the advantage of the trapped. It's like fishing with a real creative lure. It's meant to attract or seduce the fish in such a way that the fish thinks he's getting a pretty good meal for little or no cost. Such a deal, right? That is, of course, until the fisherman feels the subtle pulling of the hook, signaling him to jerk the pole upwards, thereby setting the hook deep into the flesh of the fish. If the fisherman sets the hook correctly, that fish is soon going to wind up in a net sucking nothing but air as he struggles in vain to get away, only to be met by a thudding gaff to the head. So just like that, a happy little fish thinking he was getting a free meal winds up dead.

Now don't get me wrong, I enjoy fishing and am only using this as an example. With this example, we see a fisherman who knows very well what he's doing. In fact, he's studied about lures and water condition and weather and probably even practiced his casting out in the backyard. The fish, however, is totally clueless. And, for the sake of illustration, there's probably some older and wiser fish somewhere who's tried to get this one to be really careful, but instead of paying attention in his fish school, he didn't listen and figured "that would never happen to me." So he just bumbles along, careless and ignorant. Suddenly, he sees this great big temptation dangling right in front of him and without any further thought, chomps down!

The fish, like many of us, lacks wisdom. He didn't actually stop to ponder his next step. He just reacted to a stimulus that eventually got him fried (or broiled or barbecued). Proverbs speaks often of wisdom and of being aware of traps so you can avoid falling into them. "Get wisdom," says Proverbs 4:5, "get understanding; do not forget my words or sway from them." Whose words are we to not forget? The words from God, His words as recorded in the Bible. Therefore, the wisdom Proverbs is talking about isn't from our college professor, our denomination, or even from our own family. While each of these may indeed possess wisdom, God wants us to go to the ultimate source of wisdom, Himself. And He's given us a great tool for doing just that in the Bible. Read the Bible as your first source for wisdom. It's amazing how many topics are actually addressed in the Bible, provided we just sit and read it. So seek wisdom first from the Bible, the Word of God.

This is great sounding advice, especially for one who has been raised from the cradle with biblical wisdom and is used to reading the Bible because it has been read to them since birth, or perhaps, while even still in the womb. But for those of us who were not so raised, we have a more difficult time with discernment of people and their motives because we aren't well taught in the wisdom of the Bible. In fact, we may even find the Bible confusing or contradictory. So, when someone comes along to "show" you how to read your Bible, they get your attention, but you still don't have enough understanding to realize that what they're actually showing you is simply their interpretation, or in other words, what they want you to think it says. To use the example at the beginning of the chapter, they're really only presenting their cleverly disguised lure. But we don't know any better. This lure looks very similar to that squiggly thingy I ate yesterday so this must just be like that but better. Chomp!

Thus, you are ensnared, trapped, having been hooked but good through your cheek. However, once you're ensnared in the trap, as you've read through the last few chapters, recognizing the trap is slow if not impossible, because you're now steeped in the organizational twisting of Scripture that you now perceive as truth. In fact, once so deep into the trap it's easy to think that others are wrong and are themselves stuck in a trap, particularly if they're religious and follow more rituals and routines. But, woe to anyone who tries to point your trap out to you — unless it's done in love and with gentleness. Otherwise, we never see the hook sticking out of faces. This is what Jesus refers to as a plank sticking out our own eye on Matthew 7:3. We're preoccupied with trying to get the dust speck out of someone else's eye why all along totally ignoring the plank sticking out of our own eye.

Anyway, suffice it to say we're pretty hardheaded and unlikely to pay much heed to someone we are trying to beat over the head. Softness and gentleness are much better strategies to employ. However, it always helps when the trapper begins showing his true colors.

In the last chapter we explored how the organization, by involving me in the more internal workings, began exposing themselves and their true colors of deceit. At the same time another interesting situation began developing in my life as well.

It all started by the stainless steel drinking fountain at the north end of the second floor of the Energy Building. One of our customer service staff had been invited to my house for a fellowship meeting. She was going through a divorce and had been estranged for some time and was finally able to begin mopping up the ugly details that are involved in all divorces. Anyway, at that drinking fountain we met in the hall where she asked me about the fellowship. As I looked into her eyes to answer the questions my soul jumped a bit, but, of course, I didn't know why, I certainly didn't want to get involved with someone going through a divorce rather than already being completely divorced. If anything, reconciliation with her estranged husband was preferable to anything else (she did try to reconcile but soon discovered how hopeless that was — marital reconciliation takes two).

Ah, but then God has His divine appointments in His time, and through much tribulation, we started to realize there was a chemistry between us that was based, not in lust or even love, but based in our desire to seek and know God.

You see, she to, had been disillusioned by churches in her life, only her disillusionment came from mostly one denomination.

She did eventually come to my fellowship but as she did so, she then learned more about the organization that I was part of and shared this information with her family who were not, I later discovered, spiritually or biblically ignorant. That started a firestorm of controversy as she was then realizing that the organization was not Christ-centered, but was instead, a cult. As this discovery took deeper root in her soul, she felt the Lord was convincing her to delicately inform me of this truth. She sensed that while my heart for Jesus was genuine as was my desire to know the Bible's truths, my practice, meaning my belonging to this organization, was definitely not genuine and I needed to get out.

Over the years of my life many people in no uncertain terms have told me what they thought of this organization and my involvement in it. Even to the point that in graduate school this one guy and I were on a break from class and relieving ourselves in the restroom where he stated to me emphatically between the urinals that I was going to hell for my beliefs!

"Who are you to tell me I'm going to hell?" I thought. I speak in tongues, I read the Bible every day, I know more scripture in my frontal lobe than you know in your whole brain, so just who's going to hell here?

Perhaps both of us are. Perhaps neither of us are. But the point here is you don't try to save a person from a cult by blasting his identity and pronouncing him hell-bound. I mean c'mon, how many little-leaguers have really desired to stand in the batter's box because the coach yelled out they were going to the bench if they didn't stand there and bat a run in? Not many, I'm sure. They usually think that it's easy for the coach to stand in the dugout screaming while he stands in the line of fire waiting for a kid who can't find the strike zone to throw a ball as hard as he can at his head. What's the coach thinking? A ball flies for my head and I'm gonna duck, not swing at it.

Here's another example. Blasting someone's identity and pronouncing them hell-bound is like asking someone on a date by first saying "you're stupid and you're ugly. Would you like to hang out with me for a while? Maybe we can see a movie and get a bite."

How would you answer that question? I know how I would answer it but I'm too polite to print the exact way I'd say 'no'. But I'd say 'no' in a most colorful way, if you what I mean.

Did Jesus run around saying those kinds of things? I think not. He confronted devilish men harshly, but He seemed to be pretty gentle to the stupid and uninformed. That would be you and me before we developed a close personal relationship with Him.

Janey is the dear woman whom was worried about my eternal destiny and whom, thanks be to God, I eventually married. We had a beautiful, Christ-honoring wedding in a real church conducted by a real Pastor —talk about a turn around. This was the same pastor who baptized my oldest son and me and warmly took me in to his church after I left the cult. But that's another story. It's just symbolic of the complete deliverance God can bring to a person's life as he humbles himself under the mighty hand of God (see I Peter 5:6).

Now, where was I?

Oh yes, Janey approached me with gentleness and love. She politely asked me why I believed some of the things I did when they seemed so contradictory to the Bible. So I sat down with her on my couch in the living room and began explaining these things to her. That's when I began realizing I couldn't refute the virgin birth without the writings of the organization's founder right at hand. Or I couldn't really explain the significance of three being crucified with Jesus versus five being crucified with Jesus without his writings. In other words, really reading the Bible regarding key Christian doctrine at face value, something I thought I had been doing for all these years, really started to shake me up since I was seemingly unable to explain the logic of the organization. What I thought was easy to refute as nothing more than mere tradition creeping into Christian dogma over the centuries now suddenly seemed less and less like tradition and more and more the actual words of the Bible. Could it be that…nah, I couldn't be wrong, I had spent waaaaayyyy too much time in this stuff to be wrong. I'd done deep research, filled a few bookshelves with expensive research books and even developed a familiarity of the Greek language. How could all that be wasted effort?

Needless to say I was a bit obstinate. But she persevered in her gentle but tenacious way.

Finally, through one gentle letter she really let loose a salvo for God.

"Not everyone who says to me, 'Lord, Lord,' will enter the kingdom of heaven," says Jesus in Matthew 7:21. It goes on to say:

"Many will say to me on that day, 'Lord, Lord, did we not prophesy in your name, and in your name drive out demons and perform many miracles?' Then I will tell them plainly, 'I never knew you. Away from me, you evil doer.'"

—Matthew 7:22-23

Okay, she got my attention. I was finally beginning to ponder the hook sticking out of my cheek, the plank sticking out of my eye. And she did it with love and with the Scripture itself, not with loud pronouncements of doom, or railing accusations of blasphemy, or even bringing a "Jesus Intervention Team". She did it gently, in love, and with the very words of Jesus Christ Himself.

"Then I will tell them plainly, 'I never knew you. Away from me, you evil doer."

I had to reallllllly think on this one.

"Tell them plainly."

"I never knew you."

"Away from me."

"You evil doer."

Evil doer. Me? No way. Not after all these years, sixteen and a half, to be exact. God certainly would have told me by now. Wouldn't He? I mean, c'mon, God wouldn't let me spend so many years and so much money just chasing after the wind would He? I've been following after God, right? Not after a man, right? Right?

Oh my! Slowly a dawning comprehension began cresting over the din of organizational rhetoric. My heart began palpitating again, a sweat literally began beading up on my forehead. A darkening despair started gnawing at the bottom of my heart, threatening to rip a hole in it to drain all my life's blood to my feet. I had to sit down as a realization was fighting my consciousness for attention, but I didn't want it to come to bear. I wanted to bury it, to throw her letter away and to hide from…from, from what? From myself? From her? Or, from God? Suddenly denial was really a welcoming temptation. Just deny it and maybe it'll go away, maybe the thought will become nothing more than a very realistic dream.

Still I kept questioning myself, "what am I running from?"

I couldn't tell. All I knew was I started to be filled with not just dread, but with anger and even fright. Had I been wrong all these years? All these years. What a frightening phrase, all these years. And I was raising my son with the same under-standing as me, so not only could I be wrong with my own life but leading my son, whom I'm responsible for and who trusts and respects me, down the wrong path altogether.

So I ran an inventory of crucial biblical/Christian concepts through my brain. We taught Jesus was not God. Biblical/Christian concepts taught that He was God in the flesh, God incarnate is a more familiar phrase.

We taught Mary was a virgin when Christ was conceived but not when He was born. Biblical/Christian teaching taught she was still a virgin at His birth.

We taught the dead didn't go to heaven (or hell) right away but only at the return of Christ. Biblical/Christian teaching states your soul (which some use the term spirit as synonymous with soul) goes back to God and waits to be united with your body. This embraces that the soul houses the consciousness, which means that in essence, we do go to heaven upon our death. There is no waiting, and we are aware of what's happening.

We also taught that hell was, rather than eternal, nothing more than a lake of fire where the unsaved were tossed, being instantly snuffed out of existence and even remembrance. Biblical/Christian teaching states that there is a hell, it is eternal, and aside from the fire, the smoke, the gnashing of teeth, there is also eternal separation from God. The Bible also proclaims that in hell you have consciousness and are acutely aware that you have missed, for the rest of eternity, your opportunity to be in heaven with the Lord.

And I could go on.

What about the significance of forgiveness, mercy, and grace, which we always minimized? What about the many multi-faceted giftings of the spirit rather than everyone receiving the same package? What about God's sovereignty versus our need to just believe bigger? What about just being quiet in prayer and letting the Holy Spirit wash over you rather than having a laundry list of requests and expectations of God. What about…

Suddenly I got a mental "mind-picture" of Jesus looking me in the eye and saying, "Craig? Craig who?"

Needless to say my world had been rocked like it had never been rocked before. I had to figure out a way to investigate this potentially life-changing discovery. Obviously if I've been wrong all these years I still truly desired to seek the Lord. I needed to really get a handle on what to do now and how to make it right with God if I had been wrong.

Oh my, but could I make it right with God?

CHAPTER NINETEEN

Exit Strategy

———+———

"I, loving freedom and untried;
No sport of random gust,
Yet being to myself a guide,
Too blindly have reposed my trust.
                    —*William Wordsworth, Ode to Duty.*

"He has sent me to proclaim freedom for the
prisoners."
                    —*Jesus, Luke 4:18b*

Obviously, the whole state of my spiritual life was at risk. Was I really part of a group that actually brought dishonor to Christ? Were we really teaching against the truth of Jesus? Was my grasp of biblical doctrine regarding Jesus Christ really that skewed? Could it really be true that, along with all my closest friends, I had been toiling away for all these years in vain, devoid of true joy in the absence of true deliverance? Had I been doing nothing but languishing away in a dry, desolate desert where there was no water, no refreshing, and no Jesus?

No wonder my soul ached so deeply, or that my heart was constantly casting about seeking a peace that always seemed so close yet was so elusive. No wonder I still pondered the viability of other faiths since I was still fighting the battle of an empty heart, a tired soul, and a quenched spirit.

My concerns continued mounting as I knew that if I did nothing about this greatly disturbing state of desolation, I could cause a whole lot more trouble for my son and me. If I felt so empty and lacking in joy now, what possible change could there be in my future if I merely continued on the path I was now on. If I didn't make some sort of move now, I somehow felt I would be doomed to a life of always dreaming of a state of peace that I knew I'd never attain. And, if somehow I wasn't saved, well, just the thought of not spending eternity with Jesus in heaven was more than I could bear.

Plus, I couldn't continue the thought of being responsible for not just being misled myself but for also misleading my son, my own flesh and blood. I needed to get answers and I needed to get them quick.

Somehow, though, I needed to test out my concerns that the organization may not be what I always thought it was. But how could I quietly and covertly run tests? And what sorts of tests should I run? It's not like I could just come out and say statements like "I'm concerned this may be a cult. Can you help me sort this out?" I'm sure they'd be more than happy to sort it out, right up to sending me through more confrontations of what I was thinking and why. They'd definitely determine themselves to set me straight and clean out my mind of all those wicked thoughts. How dare I even consider that they weren't the holders of God's truth?

In fact, I remember on several occasions some corps leader or another indicating that while other groups may have some truth of God's Word, no one had the complete truth like we do. Wow, is that a claim of truth, or of arrogance? I guess that's what I wanted to find out.

So for me to begin challenging the mindset "we have the all-truth," was doing nothing but inviting more unwanted scrutiny and confrontation, when what I was really being led to do was mount up a quiet fact-finding campaign.

And I certainly couldn't just say "well, Janey said she's concerned about this organization really being a cult, so I'm gonna do some checking around, I hope you don't mind." That would do nothing but precipitate the "mark and avoid" card after long drawn out sessions of why Janey was no good for me. In fact, I was already getting precursors to this conversation as it was.

I remember one person in the organization thought she needed to point out to me that Janey was no good for me because she resembled my ex-wife. What?! Evidently this was some sort of psychology 101 off-the-shelf psychoanalysis. I guess she figured that blond hair means resemblance and resemblance then means some twisted psychological desire of mine to seek nothing but a replacement for what was lost, a direct replica of what I once had. She didn't take into account that other features, such as looks, personality and interests were completely different. Nor did she consider that I had absolutely no desire to repeat all the pain and shame that came with my previous marriage. Why would I want to replicate the worst pain I'd ever been through, especially when it involved a totally innocent child?

Plus I'm not as stupid as all that. I know the real concern was that Janey wasn't one of them. She hadn't taken the class so that made her some sort of sub-human entity in the eyes of most people who had taken the class. Speaking of twisted psychology, the class seemed to take on its own identity in these people's souls —I've had the class, therefore I am.

No, for me to successfully investigate the viability of the organization, I had to think of something that would be, at least for the most part, unsuspecting; something that would be a test I could relate to and understand but that wouldn't be easy to detect with a sense of plausible deniability.

Funny, just the thought of having to run a test ought to tell me something, and, in a way, it did. I started realizing that if I truly was in a cult, how the heck would I get out of it? And while I was thinking this I also started thinking about how nice it just might be to no longer live under the clutches of people who were so uncaring but always interfering and desiring of confrontations. It was like the air they breathed, like the devil being a roaring lion seeking who he can devour. These folks were like raging opinions seeking whom they might confront —think like I do or face my wrath...and my intrusion into your privacy...and...you get the point.

But after receiving the "Janey letter", I thought more deeply about the various and disturbing events shared earlier, about how they exhibited a coldness that was nowhere near the compassion I think Jesus would show. I remember one author described Jesus as "at once sweetly accessible and altogether unknowable"[17]. I could not think of the leadership in this organization as being "sweetly accessible" since they were always wanting to state their opinion of how they thought you should live; and since they did this so often, they were quite "knowable" because of their absorption of self based in organizational identity. So I guess they would be more described as "avoidable" and "arrogantly boisterous," both attributes not applied to Jesus.

I started thinking that if they weren't showing the compassion of Jesus, then were they really honoring Jesus in the first place? And why were they insistent on being so controlling over every detail of a person's life? I remember going for runs in the park fretting over the thought of my fellowship coordinator finding out about some minor mistake of mine —and there were people definitely more than willing to bring them to her attention if given half a chance.

Even after I admitted to a mistake and knew what to do to fix it, I'd still get one of those confrontations and intruding solutions. Then I'd have to report back on my progress of improvement for weeks on end either verbally or via email. Having to continually report back on my improvement progress did nothing more but constantly remind of my weaknesses over and over again, while continually fueling her fodder against me. It was silly stuff over simple mistakes; simple mistakes we all make that Jesus Himself didn't fret much over. You apologized, you got forgiven and cleansed, and then you moved on. Doesn't I Corinthians 13, where it talks about love, state that love "keeps no records of wrongs" (see verse 5)? This sure seems like keeping a record to me.

I remember one night Nellie and I were having dinner with some friends at their house in the country. The conversations were quite transparent about our fears and frustrations of life. A little too transparent. In the next day or two I was being told by the husband that he really thought he'd better tell Tracey what I was saying. While I said some things I needed to clarify and apologize for (which I did), I was also panicked to think he'd go to Tracey, I certainly didn't want her knowing any more details about my life than she already knew, especially ones so personal. She had a knack of using your trust in her against you and she already knew more about my life and thinking then she had a right to. Plus, as cult leaders are typically prone to do, they hold all this knowledge against you as a way of constantly asserting their authority over you. And as they "lord" their authority over you, they endeavor to make you feel weak and stupid and lucky to have them there to guide you through your ignorance. In other words, they don't dispel shame, they propagate it.

Thankfully he didn't go to Tracey but having a leader I couldn't trust or confide in was also very telling —wasn't

Jesus a person to confide in? Wasn't He making intercession for us with the Father, even right now? Shouldn't those who represent Jesus be there to listen, to help, and to guide in a biblical manner if needed? Then, wouldn't someone who instead controlled, extolled guilt, heaped shame, and intruded into your privacy, really be representing something other than Jesus? And if so, then weren't they representing the opposite of Jesus? Like, the devil?

Sobering, isn't it.

All these thoughts from the past began flooding into my thinking. I began recounting all the discomfort, hurt, and intrusion both my broken family and I had endured over the years. I started comparing these with times from long ago of actually experiencing peace and deliverance, like the time earlier described at that youth camp in Canada. Now, finding that peace and deliverance again was becoming a consuming desire of my heart, my new number one passion.

So I prayed for guidance on what to do, on how to really begin seeing what was really of God and what wasn't. I spent time with Janey so I could discuss with her what some of my plans were. She thought my ideas were good, but she really wanted me to do it without her influence so I would see the organization for what it really was through my own eyes and not through any influence of hers or anyone else's. The filters of my perception needed to change on their own accord and not through the desire to please someone else or to be with someone else. No, this needed to be about what my heart was telling me via the Spirit, not what my brain was telling me in order to please others.

In other words, I needed to really strengthen my desire to seek after God and to know the truth of Jesus Christ. This desire then would fuel the Holy Spirit's operation in my life and the truth would eventually be clearly known to me.

So, let the testing begin.

Well, I guess I actually started testing the organization when I started pressing against Joe when he kept flinging flaming arrows at people in my fellowship. That was not intended to be a test but it was the old Craig coming out to challenge unfairness, injustice, and unsound thinking. Just because you're leadership doesn't always make you automatically right. In fact, good leaders listen before they speak rather than just "bulling" in with their opinions blazing like so many pistols. In essence, then, the organization was undergoing some scrutiny from me, and it was failing miserably.

But that wasn't enough for me to just chuck sixteen years of my life, sixteen years spent in pretty strong commitment to an organization that I now was seeing more and more as a cult. I needed more deliberate testing.

Since the holidays were rolling around, I thought this was a very good time to test out their intrusion into people's lives during the holidays. I already mentioned in Chapter Nine about the "Christmas/ho-ho" stuff. But here's a little more elaboration about that. They felt that the word really meant a celebration of Christ's death rather than His birth. They got to this conclusion by saying the 'mas' at the end of the word was really the Roman Catholic word 'Mass' which is typically a funeral, or acknowledgement or celebration of one's death. Thus, putting the word 'Christ' before the word 'Mass' then meant to them the celebration of Christ's death.

Really. I'm not kidding you. So, as I mentioned, instead of 'Christmas' we'd say 'ho-ho' or 'household holidays.' Just think of how much of an idiot you sound wishing someone 'happy ho-ho' on December 24th. Plus this greatly limits your Christmas card options as well!

During the last two weeks of December I decided to do a few things that were unorthodox for this organization. I would not have any fellowship meetings during that time nor would I attend any meetings —they always felt compelled to have some meeting or another scheduled during that time frame to keep us away from all the worldly rhetoric about Christmas —and I didn't schedule any witnessing events either (though I was stupid enough to attend one up in Portland where I got to watch Joe rip apart an old lady regarding Jesus Christ not being God [remember, that's what *they* believe]. He was so harsh with the poor old woman that he brought her to tears —where's Jesus in that?). But I did spend time with my family, particularly my son, and, much to the ire of people watching, with Janey.

So here's the stage: I'm not hanging out with like-minded organizational people, but I am hanging out with people of influence in my life that are not a part of the organization. This was not good in their book of how to cope with 'ho-ho' and all the holiday stuff. Soon I started getting invitations from people in my fellowship to various things —it was now their turn to test me.

Even though I had explicitly said I was going to lay low during the holidays, I kept getting invited to go do things with the fellowship. One woman, the one with the son who was resoundingly criticized, decided we should have a pizza party and that it'd be a good idea for me to organize it. I politely informed her that such a gathering was fine with me, but she needed to organize it since it was her idea in the first place, and since I was not intending on attending. Well, the gathering never materialized. It did, however, release a firestorm of criticism of me for not wanting to gather with the people in my own fellowship.

Also, a neighbor of mine was putting together a Fiesta Bowl party as one of the Oregon teams was playing in it that year. I invited the controlling husband to join us, along with Janey. I did this because I knew he was very nosey and I wanted to see what he would say. True to form, he did not let me down.

As the game ended, we went back to my house —Janey, Mr. Controlling, and I —where he felt compelled to pull me into my own study where he could talk to me alone. Uh huh, you guessed it, another confrontation.

He had very harsh words for me for not fellowshipping with like-minded believers, for refusing the pizza party (which wasn't true), and especially for hanging around with Janey. He told me he was afraid they'd lose me and that would be a terrible thing since his kids really looked up to me. If I were to leave, he said, they'd be devastated. (Translation: if I left the organization, they would really begin to question the sanctity of the organization themselves, which was dangerous, since they were both getting to the age of making their own decisions. And this could lead them to discover the truth about Jesus and the falsehoods of the organization in which dad was so deeply enmeshed.)

He said I really needed to think about the conversation and then report it back to Joe. Ah, that's it, then, isn't it!? Joe sent you. I figured as much. Big ol' Joe wasn't invited so Mr. C had to be his spy. But the spy had long sense blown his cover and was one of the crucial lynch pins in the success of my investigation, as was Joe himself.

So, as the day darkened outside, so did my mood toward Mr. C and the whole of the organization. I could feel the commitment of my soul beginning to sunset, as was my desire for giving a doggone what these people thought of me. Did they do anything to help my marriage as it fell apart in smoldering debris? Did they exhibit any forms of compassion, mercy, or forgiveness for those who had really screwed up their lives? Did they really care at all for the hurting masses of humanity surrounding our lives everywhere in the world? Or were they really about themselves, and their little enclaves into other people's lives? Were they really about protecting their own self-interests and self-proclaimed fiefdoms over other's souls? Were they really just about control, greed, and power?

I assured Mr. C I would think very hard about what he said, but I was clear that my decision was my own and that I may, or may not, inform Joe of any of this conversation, knowing full well, of course, that Mr. C would. I knew he would spin what Joe wanted to hear, that he would exaggerate my relationship with Janey and make her out to sound as bad as he could to Joe.

Then I offered to show him the door.

As he left, Janey burst out in tears because she knew the conversation was hurtful to me just by looking into my eyes, and that she was the bulk of the reason for the confrontation. I assured her she had no fault in the arrogance of others and that I was sensing that my life was about to drastically change yet again.

CHAPTER TWENTY

And the Scales Fell

——+——

I need to fly
but can't find
my wings,
Or the wind,
or…
my will.
    —*Journal entry of 12/31/01*

Immediately, something like scales fell from Saul's eyes, and he could see again.
                    —*Acts 9:18*

We've all seen the depiction of justice as a blindfolded woman holding in her hands even scales. So the story goes, she is blind so as not to render a personal opinion of right and wrong. Rather, as evidence is gathered it is to be placed on the appropriate scale. Once all evidence has been gathered, the scales are to tip to where the bulk of evidence lies, thus, signaling what is and what isn't, truth. The scales tip toward truth while falsehoods fling upward, to hopefully dissipate into nothingness.

This is how justice is supposed to be played out. It shouldn't be based on who has the best lawyer or who is the best orator, of if the jury is bent toward a prejudice or a favoritism. It should be based on the solid evidence presented. Once the evidence is presented it is then weighed for viability and substantiation. Viability meaning all can understand what is meant and substantiation meaning witnesses can verify the evidence, places, documents, or repeat experiences.

For the Christ-follower, truth is also sought for in God's Word and via prayer. The Holy Spirit can attest to truth as well or better than any gatherable evidence. The Holy Spirit working and prompting in your heart may be the best "truth-indicator" we could ever have.

As my testing of the organization began drawing to a conclusion at the beginning of the new year, God had something for me that only He could ordain and divinely appoint. And it happened at just the right time in just the right way.

It was another one of those weekly phone conversations with Joe, as it turned out, the last one I ever had with him.

But all through this process, both Janey and I were praying that God would show me the truth and that I wouldn't be swayed by Janey, or Mr. C., or Joe, or anyone else, but that I would instead have a clear leading from God of what the truth was. While my scales were definitely tipping against the organization, God had one more experience, one more exposure that would prove to be the last bit of clear and convincing evidence I would ever need.

The phone rang.

"Hello," I said.

"Hi, Craig, it's Joe." And off we went.

I won't give a blow-by-blow dialogue of the conversation since I'm not writing a script, but I will give a summation of each point in the conversation. And what a conversation it was. Both Janey and I were accused of evil, I was called a failure, I was given unbiblical commands, he mentioned that I may very well wind up dead because of Janey, and lastly, the final revealing was the doctrine he held to the highest level; the doctrine he was expecting me to abide by just because he said so, but it was doctrine not based in nor on the Bible itself.

This was the first phone conversation with Joe since Mr. C had laid down his pronouncements upon me, so I knew this would not be an easy conversation what so ever. I'd been dreading it all day long and was doing what I could to prepare for what ever he threw at me. Even so, I was unprepared for the ferocity emanating through his voice.

It started with the typical pleasant banalities of greeting and then moved into a brief rundown of all the folks in my fellowship, but in this conversation the person he wanted to focus on was me.

In just minutes, he dove into the subject he really wanted to discuss: Janey. He accused us more than once of having inappropriate intimate relations with each other. Whether this was true or not (from our point of view it was not true) there was no way for him to know how close we were or what sorts of intimacy we engaged in. But this portion of the conversation revolved around nothing more than sexual accusation. He even accused me of thinking with body parts below the neck. He gave no acknowledgement that our conversations revolved around the Bible, most especially Jesus Christ. He made no effort to even try to understand the common bond between us, which was, as I'm sure you've figured out, Jesus Christ.

He made no mention of the possibility that we may actually love each other and that perhaps God was bringing us together. No, he was just focused on sex. Hmm, his continual harping on this made me think that's what was on his mind regarding Janey, having sex with her —otherwise, why would a married man be so preoccupied with a single man's sexual intimacy? Particularly when there was no proof such intimacy was even occurring. I even wrote in my journal shortly after this conversation that I felt Joe was, from a psychological point view, projecting his thoughts onto me, and since his thoughts lingered around sex, he figured mine were as well so therefore I was sinning and committing a condemnable act of evil.

What a bunch of circular hypocrisy, projecting your own sin onto someone else who is exhibiting no sin at all (at least not in that particular topic area).

I would label this in the category of "Phariseeism," meaning Joe was doing to me what the Pharisees were doing to Jesus – projecting their scarlet sins onto the pure white of Jesus Himself. But, of course, I am nowhere near pure white except what Jesus has cleansed me from. But the point is this so-called leader was behaving just like a Pharisee; you'd think that such a self-proclaimed Bible expert would realize such a thing.

As a slight digression for a bit more background on this topic, the main leader of the organization, mentioned earlier as Carl, had been Joe's mentor plus Joe worked directly for him as well in the inner sanctum of headquarters. This Carl, as it turned out, had to resign in disgrace due to several extramarital sexual indiscretions that were allegedly reported to be forced rather than consensual (newspaper reports from the nearest local paper followed the story closely). Further, corps training compounds have long been accused of being more sexual escapades than actually schools of learning and several of the top leaders over the years, including the founder himself, had been accused of being sexual predators —using their positions as "godly" men as means of taking advantage of young women, if not girls. Their posture was evidently along the lines of "I'm the leader of God and to please me is to please God," and according to personal accounts this type of behavior was not uncommon among the organization's top leaders. (For a specific reference, begin with *Encyclopedia of Cults and New Religions*, 1999, Ankerberg, J. & Weldon, J.; Harvest House Publishers, Eugene, Oregon; pp. 612-614, 616.)

So, for Joe to be hyper-focused on sex right off the bat was not entirely surprising but still disturbing just the same. So was he viewing Janey as not a soul for Jesus but rather as a sex partner he can't have? And if so, is it driving him crazy to think I'm "getting" something he's not? I'll never know, of course, but to start a conversation by focusing so heavily on sex is questionable.

Granted, many a legitimate godly leader has been taken down by sexual weakness, so it is an issue to be wary of. But when we're talking about two single adults in an organization that didn't necessarily teach that sex was just for marriage, the context is a bit suspect; especially given Joe's close connection to Carl and his alleged long-term sexual indiscretions involved there.

So now that we've been classified as sex-crazed and therefore evil, even though there was no evidence backing the claim, nor was there any mention of the possibility of really being in love either.

With that salvo fired, he then moved into the next phase of the conversation, that being how could I "possibly consider another relationship at all seeing as how I had already failed in my marriage."

Boy, that sure felt good, as the guys in the initiation ceremony in *Animal House* cried out, "thank you, sir, may I have another!" I felt like I'd just been whacked hard and was now taking another one — and I was expected to just take it obediently and even act like it was okay.

"Why would you think you could have another relationship since you've already failed in your marriage," he asked. Hmm, what does Ephesians 4:15 say, something about "speaking the truth in love?" The truth in his statement was, at best, questionable, but there was definitely no love in that statement at all. And, yes, I did have my failures in my first marriage but I sure wasn't alone in that area nor was I the one who moved out. How dare he call me a failure in a relationship he knew nothing about. He had no idea nor made any effort to discover how badly shredded my heart was over my divorce, how I felt utterly worthless and continually felt guilt when I looked into the watery blue eyes of my son as he began crying out in the middle of the night for his mother. Did Joe have no heart at all? Was he so totally oblivious to wounds such a statement could open, or to the heaping shame that could avalanche down under the crushing remembrances such a statement could elicit? Or was this a coldly, calculated statement to break me down, similar to the Tracey tactics of conversational ambush?

After he asked such a harshly cruel question my mind wanted to bust out in a blistering retort. After all, Joe wasn't the world's biggest intellectual giant, but I thought better of it. My mind quickly calmed down, like a spiritual salve was caressing over the opening wound and I considered the comment for what it was, cheap and purposeful —Joe had laid a gauntlet of battle and he expected me to melt before it was over. But I was not going to melt, not this time. I felt a sense of strength in my soul I'd not felt before, like within me the Holy Spirit Himself was bolstering me for this battle and it was a battle He was not going to lose in spite of my own weaknesses of standing up to Joe and other such leadership.

"We all make mistakes, Joe, even you. Christ forgives, so should we."

This said to a man who was trained to employ the "mark and avoid" card whenever they didn't get their way. That's what they did to my ex-wife. If any person were over at my home when she came by to pick up or drop off our son, they'd absolutely shun her, purposefully looking away or even turning their backs on her. They made no attempt at reconciliation nor forgiveness — both foreign concepts in this organization and both attributes Christ Himself lauded most highly. Christ promoted restoration, not continual destruction.

"Maybe so, Craig, but her ex-husband may come back and kill you." Whoa! That was a low blow. Evidently mentioning Christ and forgiveness stopped the previous train of thought in its tracks so he was now boarding another train. This guy's good. His comment was based on the fact that the ex-husband had at one time exhibited stalking behaviors, even to the point of showing up at my home in such a manner that got all the neighbors' attention. But to my knowledge he never came close to ever trying or even threatening to kill anyone — so this was yet another grasping-at-straws threat.

"Even if he were so angry at her," I said, "I doubt he'd do anything so stupid — the first suspect questioned would be him and the second would be my ex — neither is so stupid nor so evil."

"You never know, Craig, evil men and seducers wax worse and worse every day." Oh yes, another tactic they use is whipping out Bible quotes on you to shake you up. I guess they feel if they quote the Bible at me I'll all of a sudden relent and fall to my knees in guilt. Silly, especially since I'm smart enough to discern when the quotes are accurately rendered versus used out of context merely to elicit reaction. But I was beginning to wonder just who was the evil one here, for the quote he threw out is from 2 Timothy 3:13 and is mostly in the context of evil people deceiving others with wrong thinking about God and Jesus Christ. Hmm.

"Whatever, Craig. But what about the fact you've had the Advanced Class and she hasn't even had the Foundational Class," he asked. "Think about it, and not only that, you're a fellowship coordinator as well — people expect you to be a leader not strayed by some pretty girl who hasn't even had the class."

What a messy comment. He was using my position against me, which, unfortunately but honestly, was where I drew some of my own identity and self-worth from. He was stating un-expressed expectations of people in my fellowship, and he was re-playing the sex card. Wow. Here were three separate themes to unpack and respond to.

My first thought was Janey had registered for the Foundational Class. It wasn't her fault the organization couldn't pull together the minimum number of students to actually have the class. And how I remember well the night we registered Janey for the class.

We were invited over to some mutual friend's house for a nice dinner followed by dessert, then signing up for the class. As Curt pulled out the registration card for her to sign, I was beginning to shake and sweat, like we were somehow forcing her to do this against her will. The feeling in my soul was a strong indicator of times to come —here was a woman I was definitely falling in love with signing up for a class I had once supported but now found myself dreading. My thoughts, as much as I tried to deny them, were how I didn't want her to take the class because I was taking inventory of my life since I first took the class —and my life wasn't what they promised. I didn't have the abundance or power the class offered. Instead, I felt cowed and corralled by despots wanting to know every jot and tittle of my life. Plus, this was the very organization that contributed greatly to the failure of my first marriage —why would I promote this?

Even though I was shaking and sweating, she signed the card, paid the fee, and thankfully never set foot into session one.

So back to Joe. I was glad she hadn't had the class, hadn't been polluted as I was with their rhetoric and distortions, but that's not what I said.

"She's registered, Joe, but she's not in control of when it actually happens." All right, smart guy, counter that!

He did, but weakly. "Even so, it's just the Foundational Class and you're still an Advanced Class grad and fellowship coordinator. You should be dating other Advanced Class grads, not new babes in the Word."

"She's no babe in the Word, Joe. She's been a Christian longer than either you or I. Plus she speaks in tongues and probably has been doing that longer than either of us as well."

"Craig, she's not an Advanced Class grad and you are." His voice was beginning to gather in a bit of a high pitch and rapid intonation, indicating I was really beginning to irritate him. To continue to do so would assure that, if I stayed in the organization, I would be put under the most intense scrutiny yet in my life, I'd constantly be under the electron microscope of the probing spies of the organization. So I was at a cross roads —what would I do?

"So what, Joe? A believer is a believer." Into the teeth of the storm!

A deep sign came through the other end, the kind of sign not of resignation but of building fortitude.

"You know perfectly well, Craig, that 2 Corinthians 6:14 says we are not to be unequally yoked together with unbelievers."

I was ready for this reference. "She's every bit as much of a believer as you and I are, Joe. Maybe even more so since she's been a Christian for so many years."

A deeper sigh. "She's not an Advanced Class grad, Craig."

"Yes, but the Word of God says not to be unequally yoked with an 'unbeliever'. It doesn't say anything about not being unequally yoked together with someone who's a believer but just hasn't had the class. The class is just a man-made thing while being a believer is the heart of the person. If the hearts are right, then they're abiding by the Word of God."

Bigger sigh, then silence. He was gearing up to let me have it.

"You're not adhering to ministry doctrine, Craig. Advanced Class grads who are fellowship coordinators should not date non-grads."

I was stunned. I could feel a sensation in my eyes that was more than just welling tears.

"Ministry doctrine," I mumbled into the phone.

"That's right. If you continue to see Janey, then I'll have to remove you from leadership, that's ministry doctrine."

"Ministry doctrine," I said again. Okay, I was really going to stir it up now, especially since he just gave me an ultimatum —dump Janey and keep my position, stay with Janey and lose it, even though I have put in years of work and training and who knows how much money.

"So, Joe, what you're telling me is ministry doctrine, something I've never seen written, is being elevated above the truth of God's Word. Janey's a believer, that's what the Word says so our relationship isn't condemned by God but you're still elevating an unwritten standard above what God says."

He didn't have the courage to respond to that, instead:

"You have a big decision to make, Craig. Either remain a fellowship coordinator and support the ministry, or stay in your relationship and lose your position. You have a lot to think about."

This time I was silent. A thousand thoughts were colliding together.

"Yes, Joe, I do."

"Think hard, Craig. I'll call you back in a couple of days and we'll talk more about this."

"Okay." I could hardly wait for that conversation.

As I hung up, my guts felt like they were trying to rumble out of my body and my head was pounding. This truly was going to be a huge decision for me, one I knew was going to change the course of my life. And not just my life, but my son's as well and quite possibly Janey's. I've encountered a lot of crossroads in my life but I felt this was going to wind up being the biggest yet —and the weird thing was I knew it. How many crossroads had I raced through without even recognizing them until it was too late and I was on the wrong road?

Hanging up the phone, my eyes welled with tears, tears of pending loss like a loved one lay dying and I could do nothing to change it, like the night my Dad breathed his last breath in my arms. The loss was indescribable, and yet the potential possibilities were equally unknowable.

As the tears fell, so did the scales.

CHAPTER TWENTY-ONE

"But Now Am Found"

———+———

"I was once lost, but now am found; was blind, but now I see."
                                    —*Amazing Grace, John Newton*

"Then you will know the truth, and the truth will set you free."
                                    —*Jesus Christ, John 8:32*

*Y*es, the scales fell. And mighty was their fall along with a free flowing of tears; tears of confusion, of anger, of determination, and of…of, what, could it be? Joy? Tears of joy! And even tears of relief.

A closed tight floodgate deep in my soul was cracking open and the waters were spouting out like the gushing of a crack in a dam. For so many years I had been stoically doing what the organization said. On the surface I was cheerfully obedient while deep in my soul I was a caldron of confusion, a festering firestorm of fear and frustration. So many times the organization had intruded into the inner depths of my life; and so many times I had let them, like I had given them entrée with a red carpet reception. I had let them in to such a degree that an insurmountable wedge had been driven between the woman who had once been my wife and the matrimonial vows I had supposedly uttered under the auspices of their so-called Christian approval.

Little did Joe know it but he had just revealed to me what I was most fearing and, frankly, most expecting. And, in a way, what I was also most hopeful for —they did NOT hold the Word of God as preeminent. Instead they held themselves and their own doctrine to be preeminent.

So after all these years the caldron of confusion and the festering frustration were proving to be bubbling up from a basis of truth. Could it be after all these years this bubbling, this confusion, this festering, was actually the agitation of the Holy Spirit Himself continually sending me messages of warning deep within my soul? For it was these very messages I had been so brow-beaten into ignoring, into believing that these thoughts and those like them were not the workings of the Holy Spirit but my old man nature instead, the flesh, and not the Spirit. For how could it be the Spirit if the messages were contrary to the organization and their messages?

Oh how the scales were thick over my eyes and to a degree, my heart. But that was changing now. The scales had fallen and my heart was cracking. Perhaps the dam was actually a hardness swallowing my heart whole, a hardness I had not, until this moment, recognized, and a hardness I had not ever wanted nor ever invited. It had just slowly over-taken me through the years of mind-numbing obedience and hangdog confrontations.

But yes, that was changing now. The hardness was cracking fast now, like the cracking of polar ice as the sun's warmth radiates over it and the waters surge below it. But this warmth from above was from The Son and the surging underneath was the Holy Spirit, aggressively gaining a toehold, then a foothold, then a total leg-up. He was plowing up the hardness while also cultivating the tormented soil beneath.

Maybe there was still a chance in my life for fruit to grow.

With my tears also flowed a verse from a famous hymn: "Amazing grace! How sweet the sound that saved a wretch like me! I once was lost, but now am found; was blind but now I see."

But once the tears subsided and the song faded, I turned my face upward, and cried out, "what do I do now, God?" It was a literal verbally cried out prayer for help, for guidance, for wisdom of what my next steps should be.

"Get out," was the response. The response wasn't an audible voice anyone else could have heard, but it was instead an inner voice accompanied by that calming warmth I first felt when I was told to put my seat belt on before the wild blowout when I was five or six years old (remember that chapter? Had I not been warned to put my seat belt on, I very well may have been killed that night!). The voice was of wisdom and protection. It was also calming and caring. (How a voice can exude calm and care, I don't know, I just know It did.)

"Get out now," it repeated, as if to make the point and then drive it home.

There was no doubt in my mind that this was the true God impressing upon my spirit what He wanted me to do, He wanted me to leave the organization in haste, just as the children of Israel, with staff in hand, were to leave Egypt in haste; or as Lot was to leave Sodom and Gomorrah in haste – don't look back, just get the heck out of Dodge.

Okay. There was no ambiguity in that command and the clarity of it stunned me. Somehow it was all becoming so obvious that it was a command either waiting to burst or was, more likely, continually bursting, but now not only had scales fallen from my eyes, but plugs had ejected out of my ears. Even without an actual picture I was still beginning to see a clear vision —a vision of escape, of freedom, and of renewal.

My next thought was something akin to nakedness. No longer will I be within the covering of this organization because I was exiting out of their covering and into...into what?

"Where will I go," I asked. I know God wants His children to be part of a household, a group, a family, and here I was preparing to leave the only spiritual family I'd ever known. Again He impressed upon my heart His direction.

"Just get out and trust that I will show you."

This was heavy revelation for me because I had never really felt this close to God in my life, but still I felt I needed more clarification.

"Just how am I going to leave?" One didn't just exit a cult unless one was actually excused by the cult itself. And since I was one of their leaders I didn't think they'd just let me go easily.

"You will know, trust me."

Jesus Christ had said "you trust in God, trust also in Me." And for the first time in my life, I actually cried out to Jesus: "I trust you Lord Jesus. Please help me get right with you. Please help me to understand Who You really are." Then, pausing, the tears began flowing again as I made perhaps my most mournful plea that night. "If I have dishonored you, please, please forgive me and please don't forsake me!" I sobbed into my hands, salty tears streaming down past my quivering lips, onto my forearms and dripping into little sops on the shag carpeting.

What else could I say? What else could I do? If Jesus Christ really were God in the flesh, God incarnate, as I was slowly beginning to realize, I had preached against that. Therefore, I suppose from a worldly point of view I had committed blasphemy, giving Jesus every right to condemn me, to turn His back on me in fact, to reject me. But would He? Could the Savior's love truly be that forgiving? Would He really welcome me back into His arms as I had been so long ago on that tree-covered island in the Canadian Sound?

But in my defense, I had done what I had done with a heart that truly felt I was obeying the truth, that I wasn't just going with the flow of popular religion but that I was really seeking out and adhering to truth, that I was truly separating myself from the "pretenders" and moving with the real Twenty-First Century disciples. That, however, is the strongest testament to the depth and skill of the deceivers, especially since many of the deceived are themselves educated and intelligent people. But good deceivers very much have the skill to so thoroughly dupe the genuine seekers that once these seekers wake up realizing the extent of their folly, they are so disillusioned. Instead of turning to the truth and to Jesus Himself, they turn to bitterness, antagonistic against the faith and even sometimes blasphemous against Jesus Christ. The passing of all the years wasted and all the money lost is sometimes too overwhelming and they sink into heaps of bitter despair. Thus is the end-result desire of Satan — utterly defeated souls that have rejected the Resurrection and the Life.

That wasn't my heart, though. I still truly wanted to know Jesus, the real Jesus. The true Jesus of the Bible and the true Jesus at whose feet the disciples fell and worshipped. But would this Jesus want to know me? Would He accept me back into His flock? Or had I so tainted my soul with unknowing blasphemy that He'd just reject me out of hand, looking over His shoulder and calling back that I had my chance but I blew it. Besides, none of this was His fault, it was mine, all mine.

But if He were to reject me, then why would He go to such clear lengths to get me to hear His voice to exit the organization? If I were just going to be rejected and cast aside, why was He encouraging me into a direction that would improve my life? Suddenly I started realizing He wasn't going to reject me. In fact, I was beginning to sense that He'd always been with me through all these years, in spite of how tormenting they were. Perhaps the truth was that I was not listening to Him even though He was talking to me. Wasn't He telling me so many years ago to check out the local church I eventually ended up going to after all? Wasn't it His voice that was warning me against making foolish money decisions regarding a retirement account, but I was convinced the voice was my "old man" as the organization had said it was? Wasn't it God Who was telling me I didn't have to take that trip that wound up stranding my family at the fringes of a hurricane on that desolate Ohio farm?

Yes, in that quick moment I was beginning to realize God had been with me all these years, but as one leaves the sea, turning their back to it to drive home; I left Him. Even though unknowingly, I had turned my back on Him, He had never left me. He was always there, and as He was crucified with His arms outstretched in agonized suffering, they were again outstretched, but this time in welcome and love and mercy. He was accepting me back, just as the one sheep in the one hundred went missing, He, the faithful shepherd, had been calling after me all these years, and only now was I popping my head out from underneath the rock which I allowed myself to be placed under. Truly, as Matthew 11:28 promises, huge burdens were lifting off my shoulders: the burdens of living up to almost impossible and totally man-made standards, no longer having to fear every time the phone rang, no longer would I have to live with the pressure of being expected to spend hundreds of dollars to travel to some distant city to take a class; no longer would I have to feel enslaved by an organization three thousand miles away!

But the reality of the moment again consumed my soul and I found myself thinking how was I going to pull this off? I was in leadership and had responsibilities I had to somehow shed. I had tithe money I had to be sure to accommodate one last time. I had a fellowship meeting in just two nights I had to either prepare for or cancel. I had ministry property I had to figure out how to return, which would prove difficult since it needed to be returned to Joe up in Portland. That was definitely a trip I didn't want to make to a person I definitely didn't want to see.

How the heck was all this going to happen? My worry gear began kicking into overdrive — how many people was this going to hurt? Would they hound me for the rest of my life? What if I saw some of these folks on the street, what would happen then? How was it going to effect my son? Would my ex somehow use this against me? Would any church ever want me as part of their congregation? Was I going to have to keep my background a secret? What about...well, you get the picture. Needless to say, we can always find something to worry about if we try hard enough.

So I took a deep breath and recalled the encounter I had just had with the Lord. I trusted that was God and I equally trusted He'd help me get extricated from this mess it took me over sixteen years to make.

Quieting my mind, I prayed for guidance on how to pull this off and began my strategy. But then I thought, wait a minute, I need to call Janey and tell her the news! I figured she'd have two strong responses: thrilled they had revealed their true colors to me, and heart-broken knowing how many years of commitment and service I had given to this organization.

Oddly enough, as her phone rang, it interrupted a prayer — she was praying for, guess who? That's right, me, because she knew this was the time I'd most likely be on the phone with Joe. She was praying specifically that I'd see and know what to do, that I would know exactly what God's will was for me and my son, and that it would be God's influence over my life, not her influence.

Perhaps the timing sounds coincidental, but I think it was God further confirming that what I experienced was Him and that He was helping me and, by the way, that He was and still is, sovereign.

I was nearly breathless as I recounted word-for-word the conversation I had had with Joe, then the electric encounter with the Lord after hanging up from Joe. It was like the words tumbled out as water down a rocky incline, rushing to its final resting place. I somehow felt that the sooner I got the words out the sooner this process would commence and I'd be able to be free for the first time in years.

CHAPTER TWENTY-TWO

Freedom Road

———+———

"Then Jesus said, 'Come to me, all of you who are weary and carry heavy burdens, and I will give you rest. Take my yoke upon you. Let me teach you, because I am humble and gentle, and you will find rest for your souls. For my yoke fits perfectly, and the burden I give you is light.'"
—Jesus Christ, Matthew 11:28-30 (NLT)

"Making this decision my sense of freedom and healing is growing —I like that."
—Journal quote from January, 2002

After talking with Janey, I felt light hearted and ready to take on the task ahead of me —exiting a cult. But what a task that was, particularly as I was desperately concerned about protecting my son through this process —more changes and more sense of loss was not what he needed at this juncture in his life. As mentioned earlier this was the only spiritual family we knew, regardless of how dysfunctional it was, so pulling away from it would be an obvious disruption leaving a void that at some point would need to be filled. Even so, the anguish they caused in my soul and the stress they invoked over my life had to have been felt by my son, so just the absence of such anguish and stress alone would, in the long run, be better for my son than the status quo. And even a void would then allow us to 'be' more than 'do' all the time. Maybe a void would then allow for quiet rest and deeper quality time together. We wouldn't always have to be rushing around to meet some deadline, report back on some demand, regardless of how frivolous, or put on airs as visitors came by because folks in the organization did have a propensity to judge how the place was decorated, what was on the walls and even what shoes I wore. (I was even once criticized for how I had tied my shoes while I was up front teaching!)

In my younger years when my soul anguished over something, I would write poetry. Now at this time in life I once again returned to writing poetry in my journal. I'm no poet, but for me, writing poetry is sometimes like praying. Maybe in a way it is praying, sort of like the Book of Psalms. It's an opportunity for my soul to let out little bite-sized chunks of thoughts, feelings, and fears. The following little ditty is but an example of the poetic struggles in my heart:

Change
The change,
The growth,
The decision —
To leave or
    not to leave.
To stay means
    to suffer.

To leave is
    the unknown
    but with potential
    and freedom.
I breathe deep.
I pray.
I leave.

Okay, I'm no Shakespeare or Donne, but hopefully there's some semblance of the struggle occurring in the depths of the soul of a man leaving sixteen years of familiarity. Even amongst the anguish and stress, it was predictable. It was a rhythmic pattern to life that brought with it the weird comfort of routine, sixteen years of routine. But leave I did and freedom I gained.

Even though it was hugely challenging, the timing could not have been better. I won't recap every detail of the week, but I do want to share a few high points that could only have been accomplished in God's timing and certainly not my own.

My conversation with Joe was Monday night and my fellowship met on Wednesday nights. On Tuesday I crafted my exit letter, which I would send via email after the Wednesday gathering. That way no one else's routine would be disrupted —at least not yet.

It was a letter that had to have a lot of editing because it started out, as so many letters do, with thoughts and feelings that were none of his business. Plus, some of my thoughts and anger and bitterness came through in unbridled rawness; I didn't think such raw emotion was either Christ-like to share nor in my best interest over the long-haul, for whatever I wrote and whatever I said would become the legacy I left behind. I knew they wouldn't let my legacy be the actual positive impact I made in people's lives or the enormous contributions of time and commitment I made over the years. Instead my legacy would be twisted to protect the ugly under-belly they had unwittingly exposed me to, thus I would be remembered for how I once stood tall for God but eventually got fooled and fell because of a woman, I would be cast as an Adam, enticed and led astray.

Oh well, someday they will all know the truth.

Anyway, I wisely gave myself two days to compose and finalize the letter.

Wednesday night at fellowship I had not scheduled myself to teach, which was great since my heart was now out of the organization and I didn't want to get up there with fake smiles and commitment. Oddly enough, Mr. C taught, and, of course, his teaching was certainly not honoring to Jesus and his demeanor to me was very stark and cold. I could only surmise that he and Joe had been conferring and Mr. C was again going about his duties as spy.

Even so, the meeting was shorter than usual by design. I had no announcements and few songs, and in less than an hour, they were all ushered out of my home —and as they left saying their good-byes, I knew it would be our last good-byes, and that saddened my soul. For in spite of Mr. C, I really loved those folks, even though I've never seen them since with one exception (she works in the same building I used to work in). And with the exception of one of them, none has ever tried to contact me as a friend to find out how I'm doing. Obviously the friendships ran only as deep as the person's organizational blood. There was no commitment of friends being friends through thick and thin. These friendships were as flimsy as gnats' wings blowing in the wind. Once out of the organization you were then nixed from friendship. That alone is enough to leave the organization, for true friends will not abandon you regardless of the decisions you make in life. Just think if Jesus was this flip-floppy with us? One day we're saved, the next day we're shunned. How crazy is that?

The following Sunday was a regional gathering up in the Portland area —the perfect place to have my departure announced. This meeting is why I didn't announce my departure on my terms in my own home. I felt it was best for my departure to be announced by Joe to the region so a few things could happen: Joe would have time to figure out what to do with the fellowship since it was the only one in Salem —that way no one would be left in the lurch; and all would hear that I am not wanting to be communicated with (because you know it would only be scathing —which it was the few times I was communicated with); and he could spin it his way as the organization always did anyway regardless of how departures occurred. Janey and I knew they would cast me as duped and Janey as seducing. In other words, they would try to convince the people that we were suffering from "devil spirit influence" and being tricked away from the "household of God." There would, of course, be no attempt at exploring their own contributions to my departure —Mr. C's intrusions and threats, Joe's heartless contempt for the people in my fellowship, the continual cursings of Joe from last Monday's conversations, or the fact that the most recent leader had been exposed as a fraud and liar, an adulterer and a swindler. No, it would be 100% my fault and the organization would paint itself as a victim and as scorned, once again gritting its teeth against yet another betrayal.

Well, lies come easily to them so why not just continue the lies. The folks would undoubtedly believe them because if the organization leadership said it, then it must be true; even though they all knew me longer than Joe and knew what I was really like. They spent time in my home and with my family, we all went to events together, we spent many hours together in various toils and triumphs; but in the end, they would still take a few words from Joe to color over all those memories and all the times we had together. With a few swift brush strokes of lies and deceit, they would reduce a decade and a half of work into nothing more than colorless forms of time and events. No emotion, thus, no connection, which would hopefully —for them, anyway, means forgetfulness.

Oh well, c'est la guerre, that's life, for them anyway. Nothing I could do to change that, and in fact, the best things I could do were to leave the organization and then to hopefully get this book published as a warning and an encouragement —both to them and to others who are susceptible to the wiles of such demons and snakes.

Also during the week I was able to place organization property —chairs and office supplies —under the over-hang of my front porch for Curt to dutifully come over while I was at the office and pick up to deliver Joe in Portland (gas, of course, would not be reimbursed). The tithe money had been properly accounted for and mailed off, my email was sent, my cell phone number was changed, and my home email was changed as well. At work (we didn't have caller ID at that time) I was allowed to let all my phone calls ring into voice mail for a week and I cleared out of my home all publications (except books used as reference for this work) and tapes —ceremonially throwing all of them into recycling or trash bins.

Further, I set aside my King James Bible, since that's all that we used, and bought a New Living Translation Bible (NLT). Very generously, I was given a New International Version (NIV) Study Bible by a colleague who knew what I was going through.

Now that I was out of the organization, I felt free but also a bit rudderless. What would my quiet times be like with no study guides or books to go through? What would my prayers be like now that I wasn't necessarily praying for an organization? How would I function without a twice-weekly gathering of "like-minded" believers? Who would I pose my theological questions to? How would I explain all this to my son?

When God says to trust Him, these are some of the more complex areas of trust.

What I told my son is we were going to take a break from the tedium that our lives had been. That we would keep more to ourselves for a while so Daddy could seek after God because Daddy was feeling a little unsure about his own walk with God. And we wouldn't be having fellowships any more in our home.

His reaction? Not what I expected. He was relieved. He didn't like fellowship because he always had to be quiet and endure subjects not directed to his age. He wouldn't have to see his Daddy always stressed out about stuff. And this gave us more free time to just hang out with each other with no one else's demands invading our "bachelor pad", such as it was.

Whoa! Praise God, my son welcomed the change and rolled through it every bit as well as I did. And to this day, he now has a stronger reckoning of Who Jesus really is more than most kids raised in a traditional church all their lives. Why? Because he was seeing the other side of a coin most people never see at all.

And my quiet times?

As it turned out, my quiet times became more about Jesus growing within my soul rather than a sense of duty or works with to-do lists of prayer requests. Favorite passages from the KJV I now read in the NLT and the NIV. And while my reference books were geared toward the KJV, they obviously crossed over to the other two versions as well since they're all the same Bible, the same Holy Writ from God, the same Greek origin.

Then I went to local Christian bookstores and bought several books to help me refine my understanding of God and of Jesus. So in essence, I was now entering into a season of great exhilaration in my life as so much learning was easily at my fingertips. I read Scripture and other reputable Christian authors at every opportunity —working out at the gym, on breaks, in the late evenings, and even through boring business meetings (this last one I don't recommend, though!).

I'd compare references of Jesus being God in the flesh to references from the organization's own writings saying He wasn't, and I found, while the writings were convincing in some areas, they fell absolutely flat in other areas.

I remember one distinct Saturday morning, my son was at his mom's and I was alone in my living room with my Bibles, my journal, and my prayers. I also distinctly remember asking Jesus to show me just Who He really is. Now while I don't recommend this as a usual practice for Scripture research, after that prayer I opened my Bible and it fell to the Gospel of John, chapter 17. I previously went over this key verse in Chapter Seven, but the verse is worth mentioning again: verse five where Jesus is praying: "And now, Father, glorify me in your presence with the glory I had with you before the world began."

My heart suddenly felt electric, like one of those shocker things you see in medical TV shows used to re-start hearts. A jolt surged through not just my body, but my soul. I felt like my hair was standing on end as electricity poured out of my being.

I got it! I really truly got it!

I ran upstairs to the book from the organization's founder that he wrote trying to disprove Jesus' deity, and looked through the Scripture reference section in the back. I wanted to see what he had to say about this verse five of John 17.

Guess what I found? This guy never touched this verse; it was nowhere to be found in the Scripture reference. How could it have been? It, as I mentioned before, is so clear about the pre-existence of Jesus Christ that you'd have to leave it out if you were trying to deny Jesus Christ's divinity. He wrote about verses four and six but omitted verse five. Why? He had to, otherwise he would destroy his own hypothesis, and he would then not be successful in his attempt of pulling Jesus off the throne of life so as to hopefully put himself there. Flat out, the evidence suggests he deliberately omitted that verse. And in administrative law, omission of fact is the same as lying and in many circumstances, constitutes fraud.

You get it? Not only did it finally dawn on me that Jesus was in fact God incarnate, but the organization's founder truly was what so many had accused him of, a fraud, a charlatan, a deceiver of great proportions.

What a day of discovery this was! Even though convinced I was right to leave the organization, slight tendrils of guilt periodically plied at the edges of my conscience, questioning if I really did the right thing, especially since I hadn't yet found another "fellowship" to hang out with. But this day, this Saturday of discovery, snipped those tendrils to their root, shriveling them in the heat of truth never again to regain their slithering creep over my conscience.

I was free!

And the complexion of my journal clearly reflects this freedom as I kept reading more and more viable references about Jesus and continued to fall on my face in prayer begging for more and more understanding. The entries in my journal now became treatises on how and why Jesus Christ was God, and how any other proclamation regarding Jesus was pure folly, if not complete blasphemy. Even non-Christian historical and archeological references were corroborating in their evidence.

After this great day of discovery I was beginning to sense that God wanted me to go to church, not any church, but one specific church. I'll not use the name here, but as I investigated this church, it was my son's mother of all people who told me I knew the pastor of the church. His oldest daughter had baby-sat my son on several occasions over the years. How ironic, the pastor of a church's daughter baby-sat my son so I could go off and do business for the organization, which, as I'm sure you know, is a cult. Wow! I think that's God's sense of humor. And perhaps in some complex spiritual way, it was also part of God's provision of protection over me and my son as He knew the day was coming when I would come back to Him on my knees.

So, now this church, as big as it was, didn't seem so distant, but I still wasn't sure.

Then another great occurrence on yet another Saturday. Janey and I were having coffee in a local café on a late Sunday morning. In walked a former neighbor of mine. We chatted briefly and then I asked where'd she been that morning. At church, of course. Which one? The one I felt God leading me to.

Okay, this was weird, but we talked a little bit about it and then she gave me her copy of the sermon notes from that morning. Another moment of being blown away! The sermon notes from the Pastor were on a subject I'd been recently exploring and he was using the same two Bibles I was using —the NIV and the NLT!

This was no coincidence! God was calling me to this church sitting just east of the middle school, within walking distance from my house.

God wasn't just calling me to a church. He was calling me to be under a specific ministry, the ministry of a pastor — yes, the one whose daughter baby-sat my son —because his ministry was where my heart would be healed and my gifts restored.

It was at this church that God allowed me once again to begin proclaiming His Word through teaching and leading groups. For on that fateful and painful Monday night with Joe, I had promised God that if He ever allowed me to teach again that I would take every opportunity to teach the truth about Jesus Christ. Hence, this book. I've now had the chance to proclaim Jesus to hundreds of people from church settings, to small groups, to large gatherings, to rescue missions, and most importantly, to my sons (as this book has been written Janey and I have had the wonderful privilege of giving birth to a healthy, robust baby boy). And I've had the privilege to lead several people into a relationship with Jesus Christ!

It was at this church that I learned so much of what church is, and what church isn't (for more on that, another project of mine, *From Religion to Relationship*, will impart that learning). I have been in leadership positions and have recently been part of a core group of men who God used to found another church in this town.

Man, when God restores a soul, He goes all out! There is nothing like the freedom road of Jesus Christ who clearly declared that "I am the way, the truth, and the life; no man comes unto the father but by me" (John 14:6).

May freedom be yours in Christ!

CHAPTER TWENTY-THREE

So, What About This Church?

——+——

"Let us not give up meeting together, as some are in the habit of doing, but let us encourage one another."

—*Hebrews, 10:25*

Okay, now I'm back in mainstream church, so what? Do genuine life-transforming events really happen in church? We hear that they do, but how much of this is just hype and how much is really true?

Well, frankly, I had my doubts even at this point that I'd really encounter God in a church. Thankfully God wasted little time showing me how unfounded my doubts were.

In fact, some of God's greatest work in my life has been in conjunction with the local church of which I am now a very active member, including being a ministry director (otherwise known as a lay pastor, who'd of thunk it, me, a lay pastor!).

The main key is being a part of a real and vital church that is soundly based on the Bible and in the truth of Jesus Christ. Such a church can be an absolute oasis of life for the desolate, destitute and distraught soul. Such a church not only literally saves lives, but then introduces the needy masses to the invitation of eternal life made available only through Jesus Christ.

Here are some real-life examples.

I remember very vividly being in a prayer community service on a Wednesday night with a lovely woman who would eventually become my bride (that would be Janey), standing with me as the music began to play. As the worship music was fully engaged in a great old song, I had my eyes closed, my head bowed, and my hands raised: I hardly ever raised my hands up to that point, but to me it was the symbolic surrender of myself, and welcoming invitation to be filled with His Spirit. Then, out of nowhere, my tears unleashed like a bursting dam. I was sobbing like a baby, blowing my nose and tearing through three tissues in a manner of minutes.

What triggered such emotion? Surely I was over the hurt of my divorce, the pain of seeing my son crushed, clinging to my legs pleading with me not to leave him at latchkey alone; "Daddy, Daddy, please don't leave me, please don't leave me!" he would shriek. Surely I had come to grips with betrayal and years lost to a pseudo-Christian organization, otherwise known as a cult. Surely I had grappled with my brokenness, relenting and releasing to the only healing power that remained —love found only in Christ. I was in a new church with a vital and compassionate pastor, a congregation with more genuine hearts than I had ever seen, a healing and healthy son, a solid career, and a beautiful woman in my life. After some rocky years, things were finally looking up.

I had sought counseling, read more books in one year than I had in four years of college, and really had a healthy lifestyle going on. I was absorbing accurate Christian doctrine at a rapid rate and belonged to a vibrant small group of men who not only exhibited Christ, but also acted as my mentors. Again, things were really looking up.

So what happened?

What ever it was I just let it flow. It felt so good, like my soul was coughing up some sort of lingering crud that had finally broken loose along the lining of my heart. My girlfriend, soon to be fiancée, was looking at me with dread, I knew she thought I wasn't completely over my divorce —but I knew I was. As the congregation bowed their heads in prayer, the pastor asked for folks to seek out and lay hands on someone who looked like they needed it. My girlfriend already had a hand on me and another man, Steve, laid hands on me. They just prayed for God's peace in my soul. They didn't ask questions, blurt assumptions, use the words 'ought' or 'should', but just gently placed their hands on me, as delicately as if they were handling a soul (which they were!) and just prayed —no judgment, no preconceived prayer litany, just prayed for peace, His peace to caress my soul and heart.

And it did! His peace washed over my soul, enveloping my heart in healing waters, and it was growing as people around me touched me and prayed for me —people I didn't even know reached out to pray for me, to engage in unity in Christ with me, to care for me, to love me. The peace was indescribable, but still I sobbed wracking and wrenching sobs.

When the service was finally over, I was exhausted, my body felt lighter but sore, just like after a long run with lots of fresh air and loads of endorphins coursing through my veins! As we were leaving people smiled at me and talked with me, but no one pried, no one dug into why I was sobbing so much. They just knew God was doing His work in my life and it was no business of theirs. They just accepted me and accepted that God was beginning to have His way in my life. I was not embarrassed or humiliated. I felt loved and energized. Nowhere else but a Bible-believing local church could this event have occurred.

But even if people did ask why the tears, I still couldn't answer why. I just knew I felt good and had a growing confidence that God was real, and that He was really working in my life, in my very heart and soul! After all those years, He still accepted me, and not just that, He welcomed me with open arms of love and warmth that are indescribable. Those of us who've allowed Him into those depths of our souls, our secret closets of shame and guilt, have a silent understanding of what such love and warmth feels like. It is truly a peace that passes understanding, thus passes our ability to adequately describe (see Philippians 4:7).

The next Sunday, the pastor mentioned in his message that sometimes the Spirit just brings tears for apparently no reason. But those tears are meant to cleanse the depths of the soul. Such tears should be encouraged and welcomed, but never stifled or shamed. In fact, his exact words were "there is healing power in praise. Have you ever come into a church service when you were down, and the music started and the tears came? That's the work of God's Spirit bringing emotional healing to your life" (Pastor Barry Braun, message notes, July 6, 2002).

Apparently God knew what I didn't, that I needed more emotional healing. And that kind of healing doesn't happen alone in a vacuum. It happens when a group of broken people lay their life at the foot of the Cross, worshiping the one who died and rose again for them. It happens in the church, not in the living room, not in the small group, not in the gigantic arena, but in the local church, where God can work in a community wholly focused on Him, a community of people who you see at the grocery store, the gas station or the gym, a community that says, "Yes, You Holy Spirit, you are welcome here! Shape us, mold us, make us like You." It's a place to seek His purpose for your life and to let go of your own futile attempts to claim significance. He gives significance, we only attribute folly and vain attempts to our own purposes in the absence of His significance. When we seek our own significance it is based in fragile ego and temporal accomplishments. When we seek His significance for our lives it is based in the eternal, in His accomplishments that will endure forever, His identity of complete success and resurrected life.

It was also in this church where I was baptized, yes, immersion in water and the whole bit in front of a whole bunch of people. You see, even though I had done my best to be a Christian up to this point, I learned there was so much I had done wrong, so much that was just plain skewed in my thinking. Yet, God had forgiven me, and not only that, even got me deeply connected with very strong Christians, men and women who would exude Christ but not dilute His message nor minimize His rightful position of deity.

So, as the invitation to be baptized came around, I was prompted in my heart to do this. And do it I did. I invited my whole family, old friends, even my ex-wife, because I knew it would be an important event for our son. My ex-in-laws were there, as were my soon-to-be future in-laws. My new church buddies and colleagues from the office came. I asked friends to video tape and take snapshots. I was going to publicly proclaim my life for Jesus Christ and I was not ashamed of who knew it, who accepted it, and who rejected it. I just wanted to be close to Him, my Lord and my Savior.

As I climbed into the tank of water, otherwise known as a baptismal, I could see my little boy had tears in his eyes, so did my Mom and my fiancée. As the pastor prepared to baptize me, he talked about our many discussions in the spa at the local health club, discussions about Christ that were overheard by many. He talked of my burning desire to know and live Christ. And he said if anyone wanted to see genuine Christianity, they just needed to look at me. His words ignited my soul. Here was a man who I (and many other people) love and respect, extolling words of affirmation and praise on me! Nothing like this had ever happened to me before. At college graduation I was just average among thousands of other averages, in sports the little stars always went to someone else, in singing the little gold notes always went to someone else, and at work there was always someone else I should try to be like. But here, soaking wet in a baptismal in front of hundreds of people, I was accepted for being me! I was special, I was affirmed, I was made whole. In Him, I was significant!

And all of this solely because of God's infinite grace and mercy.

That's the local church working as God intended, at least a healthy local church —they're out there, you just have to look, and pray. God will not disappoint you. If you really want Him, He'll find you —you just have to ask! And don't be surprised that, as God brings you to a local church, He may be bringing you to more than just the church. He may be bringing you to be under the covering of the ministry going on in that church. So if it isn't the church right down the street, have faith, because God'll put you where you need to be to get the most healing and the most opportunities to give back.

CHAPTER TWENTY-FOUR

Lingering Stuff

———+———

"I am the way and the truth and the life. No one comes to the Father except through me."
                                    —*Jesus Christ, John 14:6.*

While I live in freedom in Christ, there are just a few lingering oddities in my life that are left over from those cult days —stuff you may encounter with other "cult-exiters", so perhaps this Chapter will be more of a "how-to-help-them" chapter rather than anything else (or, if you're one yourself, perhaps you'll note you're not alone!).

For example, I think one of the greatest recent inventions of mankind is caller ID. Why? Think about it. Where did most of the cult-induced pain in my life start? Via phone calls. Whether from Tracey or from Joe or from someone else, the phone was always the instrument of delivery for most of the initial salvoes discharged against me, followed up of course, by the face-to-face confrontations.

Yes, in the "olden" days I would screen my calls through the answering machine, but once this was discovered I was, yep, confronted for it —no surprise, huh! I was to answer the phone as quickly as possible because you never knew who it was or what the need was. Yeah, yeah, it was usually someone feeling like they "needed" to drop bombs on my life or to set me straight in how I did something differently then they did —I needed confrontation to comply.

I'd always answer the phone with a very tentative "this is Craig." Then I'd suck air into my lungs and hold it until the person announced who they were. If it was one of my family members I'd breath out a sigh of relief. I would even feel more comfortable talking to my ex-wife then one of "them". But, if it was one of them, especially Joe or Tracey, I'd exhale heavily as my shoulders drooped and my knees started feeling weak. Then the butterflies would begin doing circles in my stomach and I'd need to pace around with my cordless handset. While I was pacing, I was just bracing myself for what ever exploit of control was coming next. And all through this was that nagging voice whispering that this wasn't how life was supposed to be lived. Where was joy in ulcer development? How was the abundant life found in fearing phone calls?

Still to this day, when the phone rings I am immediately suspicious of who it is and of what they want. If you want to get my heart rate jumping, just ring me up on the phone, especially after the sun has gone down! Silly, I know, but still true.

So as much of a relief as caller ID is, it brings with it a new variety of anxiety. Ready for this?

Whenever one of the leaders from our current church calls I get nervous, my first thought is still "now what am I in trouble for?" My mind immediately begins racing through recent events to pinpoint where this salvo is going to come from —was it something I said or did, or was it something I didn't do, where was it going to come from? And how long would it take before I could get off the phone?

Again, this is silly, I know, Janey keeps telling me that. Never in all the times when my Senior Pastor, also my friend, calls, have I ever been raked over the coals. And the leaders who are truly in Christ are warm and encouraging people. They're fun and uplifting to talk to, never a downer. Now don't get me wrong, when there are problems, they deal with them, but let's face it, how many serious problems worthy of intense confrontations occur in a person's life? Certainly not on a weekly basis, which seemed to be the case in the cult. So in Christ-followers where people are genuinely godly, such situations are rare and widely spaced. They're also much better handled because the condition of the person's heart is what is of concern, not the image of the organization or the leader in charge.

Genuine leaders in Christ are not looking for battles, because when you look for something specific, especially something negative, you usually find it, no matter how far-fetched or fabricated you have to make something to get to what you want. It's just like the big bully at school or crawling through the bars and taverns. If they're looking for a fight, they usually find it and its usually unprovoked. It's just like little demons drive them on until they somehow cause mischief. Hmm, doesn't Proverbs speak to just that type of person —the person who isn't able to sleep soundly until they cause mischief or cause someone to fall? Why yes, yes it does to speak to that, very plainly in fact in Proverbs 4:16. Interesting tie-in here, isn't it!

In fact, this organization was so into confronting people that the former leader, the screaming Carl, even coined a phrase that was repeated throughout all levels of the organization: "confront the world with the Word." Sounds noble, of course, and they wanted to make people think that "word" meant the Word of God, but, as you have recently discovered, they really confronted people with their own doctrine, "ministry doctrine" as Joe so aptly called it.

So not only did they completely twist the Bible, they then took their twists, their ministry doctrine, and beat people over the head with it over and over again. There's that interesting tie-in again — an organization, whose leader teaches to seek confrontation paired against passage of Scripture that states those driven to cause such mischief are devilish. And even Jesus said in Matthew 5:9 that "blessed are the peacemakers". Being beat over the head with what is ultimately false doctrine is not peaceful to any degree. So the organization is definitely not seeking peace when they deliberately seek to confront people, particularly when their confrontations are so harsh that people develop ulcers and old ladies are brought to tears.

Then you have to ask yourself, "Did Jesus beat people over the head with God's Word?" No! And if anyone had a right to, it would be Him seeing as how He was the Word in the flesh and all. Jesus was, and still is, gentle. In fact, in Romans 2:4 (KJV) we see that it is the goodness of God that wins people to repentance and in James 3:17 (KJV) the Word is referred to as being easy to be entreated. It is not a sledgehammer nor a battering ram.

Okay, next item on the lingering list of oddities.

Shoes.

Come again?!

That's right, shoes.

This organization seemed to have some sort of a shoe fetish.

I started discovering this back in the early nineties. I already mentioned the "witchy" shoes. But what about the woman's husband, the leader I reported to at the time? His shoe obsession was with my shoelaces! I wore clean tennis shoes with the laces untied – that was cool then and its cool now, but not to him. He said I should tie my laces when I was teaching the Word of God; he said it looked sloppy and didn't portray the neat look I should have. Oddly enough he never said a thing about the fact I was wearing jeans as well, apparently denim was okay but untied shoe laces were not.

But my shoe saga doesn't end there.

They continually hated my German-made sandals, even though they were probably more authentic to what Jesus wore than the vinyl and canvas tennis shoes they wore. And they flipped out when I bought clogs. What a firestorm of criticism that brought. Of course, each pair of these disliked bi-ped holders invoked upon me a confrontation of severe comment, if not complete rebuke. It's like instead of having some sort of a book burning party they wanted to have a shoe burning party, but they were always my shoes and never their own —evidently I must have missed the memo regarding approved ministry foot ware!

But is foot ware anywhere connected in the Bible with someone's salvation? Hmm, no, I don't think so. I never see Jesus fussing about foot attire and the New Testament doesn't seem to usher in any creeds dependent upon shoe styles. Even at the Council of Nicea in 325 A.D. when they were dealing with such weighty matters regarding Christianity, foot ware somehow never made it on their agenda. When Martin Luther was hit by that bolt of lightening did he jump up exclaiming, "that's it; it's the shoes!" No, he came up with an understanding that it is by faith we trust in God, not by shoes. And did the great Reverend Billy Graham anywhere ever mention shoe attire in his alter calls? Nope, don't recall that he ever did.

So now when you see me at church sock less, or wearing river sandals, or my beloved clogs, just remember that it is a statement of freedom, a statement that these are my feet and I'm shod with my shoes of choice. So if you make comments about my foot ware and I seem a little defensive, hopefully you'll cut me some slack! But don't be surprised to see me still showing up with the same pair of shoes again.

After shoes there's the little concept of time. Somewhere I mentioned that the organization considered being "on time" as being ten minutes early for what ever event it was —whether a class, or a hook-up, or even the many fellowship meetings. Granted, as also previously mentioned, I'm not known as "Mr. Punctuality." Even so, the continual stress of attending all those events and having to be ten minutes early to each one has skewed my approach to time.

After leaving the organization and joining the local church, I'd stress myself out if I were nearing being "on-the-dot" on time. But as this frequency picked up and no one got on my case for it, I started to relax.

Now don't get me wrong. While it was nice to be able to relax and let life just sort of happen, I started to get a bit lackadaisical and even started showing up late now and then. Okay, I'm not so selfish to think that showing up late all the time is okay, because in fact continual lateness shows either a lack of respect for those holding the meeting, or a major lack of time management. But after so many years of having "being on time" lorded over me I noticed I started being late for the simple reason of "because I can." Look, I thought to myself, I can be late and I don't get a glare, a terse comment, or any intense confrontation. I can be late and the world doesn't stop spinning on its axis, I don't all of a sudden stop breathing, nor does lightening strike me to ashes. I can be late and discover that the event started without me anyway.

Wow, what a concept! I really enjoy realizing that watches don't revolve around me and that if life does happen — traffic jams, sickness, or another priority — I can be assured that human history will not be adversely affected by however I respond to that happenstance. In other words, I'm free; free to choose whatever course of action I deem necessary, and if that means I'm late or don't show up at all, I'm not castigated or ridiculed. Life will indeed go on.

This is particularly freeing for me since I'm more of an "ish" sort of person anyway. Being at work by 8-ish can be anything from five till to five after, and as a boss, I'm okay with that. I guess that's because I was previously held to an on-time standard that caused more stress in my life than the actual event ever alleviated. Just think about that. Placing so much stress on individuals and families only succeeds in breeding irritability about being pressed for time, which eventually leads to friction, then to disunity. And in households and families today, disunity is definitely what we don't need, and we most certainly don't need it in the church.

So the next time you set a deadline for someone, be gentle with them if they're late. Allow people to just live their lives and have some breathing room to allow life to happen. Maybe in so doing you, too, will realize that life doesn't ebb and flow on your clock and that you can relax and enjoy this gift of life the Lord has given us.

I guess a final holdover would be the continual reliance by organizations of all types, especially churches and para-church organizations, on classes or programs to make people's lives better. It's almost like they want to make us think there's a secret code revealed in the classes unlocking all the mysteries to life and happiness.

If you've read this far, I'm sure you understand how my body just tingles with concerns when someone mentions "the class." It doesn't matter what "class" it is, I am just very nervous and agitated when I see well-meaning folks using statements like "you'll learn all that in the class," or "the class will help you get healed," or other similar statements.

While I know there are many classes and seminars out there that are definitely highly beneficial and do indeed provide useful tools and life-skills for people, it is the Lord Who heals. It is Jesus Who is the primary conduit to restoration, not a class, or seminar, or specific teacher. It's Jesus, plain and simple.

And we learn of Jesus in the Bible, the Word of God. All other resources for class materials, or books, or lectures, are helpful tools for deepening our understanding of Jesus and of God's Word. But if they, the seminars or teachers themselves, begin promoting they're "all that" or that they have all the answers to life, health, and healing, then we definitely have a problem. And when attendees or devotees extol the praises of the seminars or the teachers, then what they communicate to folks like me is this person is their own personal guru. Or the class or seminar is seen as a stage of enlightenment rather than a tool for bringing Jesus into more relevancy in people's lives.

Since I've left the organization I've taken several classes and seminars, and have certainly read many books, but I continue to be cautious before I give my whole-hearted support or even become a facilitator for them. In one situation, a seminar was very helpful to me and I learned great truths that helped deepen my understanding of Jesus and better grasp my freedom in Christ. However, the originator of this seminar has later in his years begun preaching concepts from his pulpit that are marginally biblical and not completely Christ-honoring. In fact they could almost be viewed as oppositional to Jesus' message of love and forgiveness. What's more, this same individual has said from his pulpit that this marginal message should be carried by his supporters to their local pastors to bring changes to the churches throughout the country!

When Janey and I first heard this teaching while driving to the Oregon Coast, we were stunned to hear him say that, basically, divorced people should never again re-marry. To do so was sin. This completely bypasses all that Jesus said about allowable divorce, which was even expounded upon by the Apostle Paul in First Corinthians. When we got to our hotel we looked through our Bibles and could not find this message anywhere and he seemed to conveniently leave out specific biblical references with this message in them. The most disturbing part, though, was he said he was convinced God gave him this message and he wasn't going to accept anything different, regardless of what anyone might say. And a man whose ministry we supported in deed and in donations stated this. Needless to say, we stopped supporting him. Not going to go down that road again!

But imagine how we felt considering we had both previously been married and were married to each other by our Pastor who had never said we were disallowed to be remarried (an obvious statement, I know, because if he thought otherwise he wouldn't have married us!).

When I described this message to my own pastor, the word "arrogant" was spoken. We also spoke of how dangerous such suppositions were because this could very well be how cults begin!

So, even in so-called mainstream Christianity, successful seminar designers and authors can step too far with their God-given authority. So, caveat emptor, "buyer beware." And also beware of wholesale support of a specific seminar or teacher, because you never know how far they really are from that ledge of luring them into launching their own cult.

Jesus is the way, the truth, and the life. There is no other way. Regardless of how eloquent, how articulate, or how intelligent anyone may be or thinks they may be, Jesus Christ is the only way to the Father. And never let anyone try to get you into thinking they have the only truth left in the world. We are all encouraged to be like the Bereans, who "received the message with great eagerness and examined the Scriptures every day to see if what Paul said was true" (Acts 17:11). In other words, if it doesn't line up with the Scripture and with Jesus Christ, it's probably wrong.

CHAPTER TWENTY-FIVE

A New Day Always Dawns

—✝—

"The most effective work...is done by ordinary Christians fulfilling God's calling to reform culture within their local spheres of influence —their families, churches, schools ..."

—Nancy Pearcey, Total Truth.

"The Lord is compassionate and gracious, slow to anger, abounding in love."

—Psalms 103:8.

"Let the little children come to me, and do not hinder them, for the kingdom of God belongs to such as these."

—Jesus Christ, John 10:14.

It is difficult to figure an appropriate conclusion for this book. I guess the book is full of warnings but a little review probably won't hurt.

Number one is beware of any group denying the deity of Jesus Christ. If this error is their primary basis for their ministry, then virtually everything else that spins off from that will be in error as well. So the deeper you go into such a group the more enmeshed you'll become in their error, or, more bluntly put, in their lies.

As we consider this, we need to deeply reflect upon the words of Jesus Himself in John 8:44 when He plainly speaks to the devil as being the "father of lies." So if a primary premise of an organization is based on a lie, then who is it that controls the inner workings and desires of the organization at its roots? It is certainly not Jesus and certainly not a man or woman who truly wants to know Jesus. Therefore, taking Jesus at His word, we know the organization is being controlled by devilish influence. And what is the devil trying to promote at the expense of everything else? Himself (see Ezekiel 28; Revelation 12 & 13 and 18-20; and page 43 of this work). The devil is about pride and "I will do" this or that. He is the great deceiver "who leads the whole world astray" (Revelation 12:9). So an organization built upon lies and deceit is an organization built upon a satanic foundation. Therefore, anything spinning off from that foundation is, due to its origin, devilish.

A quick barometer to employ as guidance is to ask a person from any organization or religion what they think about Jesus Christ. By their answer you'll know very quickly if they're something worth pursuing. If they say something like Jesus was a good man or a good teacher or one of many prophets, but nothing about Him being God in the flesh, then, as far as Christianity is concerned, they are promoting lies and not the truth of the God who created the heavens and earth.

Secondly, there are umpteen examples in the Gospels of Jesus promoting peace and umpteen more in the New Testament promoting peace as well as joy and grace. If your organization is caught up in legalism or bondage —bondage of responsibilities or things you should be doing all the time —then perhaps they have missed the understanding of the freedom in Christ and are really more caught up in works. And organizations caught up in works are organizations caught up in themselves and in their image. Neither is of Jesus. Jesus directed everything back toward the Sovereign God, of whom He was in the flesh. If Jesus isn't central, Jesus isn't the basis.

Thirdly, if your organization is more about their own publications or books or continually claiming they are the only ones who have the truth, then they are again all about themselves and about isolating you away from the truth. And the real truth, the absolute truth of life and living is learned primarily through the Scripture Itself and through reliable teachers of Scripture and the leading of the Holy Spirit. So if the Bible sits on the shelf or is hardly referred to at all, chances are the organization is really a thin veneer of Christianity hiding a solid core of selfishness and deceit. And as we just saw, the "great deceiver" is Satan, so the organization steeped in deceit is again, devilish.

And, finally, as Jesus clearly teaches John 16, the Holy Spirit will "guide you into the all truth" (v. 13). So if you've accepted Jesus Christ as your Savior and Lord, the Holy Spirit lives in your heart, or, as is often spoken of, indwelt in the very core of your soul. And as He indwells in your soul, He will guide you into all truth through a variety of ways —as Jesus says in Matthew 3, He moves like a wind —so it is hard to say how He will work in your life, but seeing as how God is sovereign, He will work in your life in unmistakable ways. That said, then, if you are listening to a teaching or are engaged in a conversation where someone is trying to "convert" you to their way of thinking and all of a sudden you get a knot in your stomach, or a visual stop sign behind your eyes, or some other warning sign, don't do like I did and ignore it. Rather, investigate it. Stop and pray for understanding. This could very well be the Holy Spirit Himself keeping your from doctrinal and spiritual harm.

Therefore be as attentive as you can to the inner workings of the spirit as He moves and grooves in your inner being. This, of course, takes practice and studying, but in time, it will come. Meanwhile, do your best to hook up with a local church with Jesus Christ at its center and the Bible as its primary standard of life and practice, and you'll do just fine. And as the truth binds more and more into the depths of your soul, just think what kind of an impact your life will have on the sphere of influence you live in!

Now, if you haven't accepted the Lord in your life, it is simple. Just take this class on...just kidding!!! Seriously, though, it is very simple, just pray the following prayer, and after that, read Romans 10:9-10 (it is following the prayer):

Lord Jesus, I know I am a sinner and I cannot do enough in this life to deserve eternal life. But I know you have conquered the grave and were raised from the dead. So I pray now with my whole heart and soul that you come into my life, that you will fill my heart, and that you will become the Savior and Lord over me. Thank you for your forgiveness, your grace and your mercy. Amen.

Wow! Feel any different? Well, if you're like most people, probably not. But that's okay, because walking with the Lord is just that, a walk; we put one foot in front of the other and just move through life with Him at the helm. As you prayed that prayer, provided you really meant it to the best of your ability, Jesus entered your heart and you are now destined to spend all of Eternity with the Lord and you are now the living temple of the Holy Spirit —amen!!!

Congratulations and blessings to you and yours!

*That if you confess with your mouth, "Jesus is Lord,"
and believe in your heart that God raised him from
the dead, you will be saved. For it is with your heart
that you believe and are justified, and it is with your
mouth that you confess and are saved*

Romans 10:9-10

For Further Reading

———✝———

*R*eliable resources on cults (not exhaustive, there are many, many more, these are just ones I've read and recommend):

Encyclopedia of Cults and New Religions, John Ankerberg and John Weldon, Harvest House Publishers.

Handbook of Today's Religions, Josh McDowell and Don Stewart, Thomas Nelson Publishers.

Kingdom of the Cults, Walter Martin and Ravi Zacharias, Bethany House Publishers.

Reliable resources on learning more about Jesus Christ, His deity, and science (again, not exhaustive, just ones I've read and recommend):

The New Evidence That Demands a Verdict, Volumes I & II, Josh McDowell, Thomas Nelson Publishers.

More Than a Carpenter, Josh McDowell, Tyndale House Publishers.

The Case For Christ, Lee Strobel, Zondervan.

Mere Christianity, C. S. Lewis, William Collins Sons & Co.

Darwin's Black Box, Michael J. Behe, Touchstone.

Endnotes

——+——

1   End Notes

While the context of this passage is in regard to the Babylonian king, it is also in reference to Satan by comparison of the fleshly king's with the spiritual pride of Lucifer and the resulting effects for both.

2   *Jesus Christ is Not God*, Weirwille, V. P.; American Christian Press, 1975. Here's a hint, if the organization publishes its own books, question why no one else would.

3   Two sources to continue with this research are *Encyclopedia of Cults & New Religions*, Harvest House; and *Handbook of Today's Religions*, Nelson.

4   *Jesus Christ is Not God*, Weirwille, V. P.; American Christian Press, 1975, pp. 87, 91, 93-101.

5   *Encyclopedia of Cults and New Religions*, Ankerberg J., & Weldon J.; Harvest House, 1999, p. 298. I highly recommend this book.

6   Ibid., p. 129.

7   *Webster's New Collegiate Dictionary*, G. & C. Merriam Co., 1981, p. 264.

8   *Roget's Super Thesaurus*, Second Edition, Writer's Digest Books, 1998, p. 144.

9   *An Introduction to Intercultural Communication*, Condon, John & Yousef F., Macmillan Publishing Company, 1975, p. 180.

10   Weirwille, V. P., *The Way Magazine*, September-October 1975, p. 19.

11   Weirwille, V. P., *Receiving the Holy Spirit Today*, p. 148, cf. pp. 43, 126, 157, 201, 212, 225, 237, 252.

12   *Network, The Right People in the Right Places for the Right Reasons*, Bugbee, Bruce; Cousins, D, Hybels, B; Zondervan, 1994, p. 25.

13   Blackaby, Henry, T. & King, Claude V., *Experiencing God*, Broadman and Holman Publishers, 1994, p. 75.

14   Elena Whiteside, *The Way, Living in Love* (New Knoxville, OH: American Christian Press, 1972), p. 178.

15   For more on personality types, see *Please Understand Me II*; Keirsy, David; Prometheus Nemesis Book Company, 1998.

16 For more information on physical and mental hurting, read *Where Is God When It Hurts?*, Yancey, Philip, Zondervan.

17 Wangerin, Jr., Walter; *Jesus*, Zondervan, p. 108.

Printed in the United States
83841LV00002B/37-117/A